The
Gateways
Diaries

Distributed in the United States by:

FELDHEIM PUBLISHERS
200 Airport Executive Park • Nanuet, NY 10954
www.feldheim.com

Typography, Design and Printing by:

TNT DESIGN GROUP
25 Philips Parkway • Montvale, NJ 07645

Email: tomer@tntDesignGroup.com
Tel (201) 391-5392 • Cell (845) 826-0484

Printed in Israel

I

To the Reader

In the pages that follow, we meet a fascinating array of men and women who speak unabashedly in their own distinctive voices. Each offers an intimate glimpse of people and events—and the wrenching inner struggle—that were the stepping-stones in their odyssey of return to their Jewish heritage.

The "Diaries" were written over a period of several years. In view of the sensitive nature of the material, people's names, residences, job titles and other biographical data have been altered, and similar accounts were occasionally blended. As the narratives were prepared for publication, we tried to obtain updates on as many stories as possible. Not always were we successful. What became of little "Pearl" and her elderly adoptive grandparents, racing against the clock in *Last Chance?* Where is long-haired "Hal" of *A Heartbeat Away*, who so movingly sang the haunting Chasidic *zemiros* of his youth to hushed participants at a Gateways *melaveh malkah?*

To the breathtakingly honest, courageous figures who people this book, I offer my deepest thanks for sharing with me intensely private excerpts from the pages of your lives. Your respective sagas, with all of their captivating twists and turns, have inspired and enriched me, as I'm sure they will countless others.

May Hashem grant each and every one of you success and happiness on your journey, and may He bless us all with the greatest gift in His emporium: the ability to use our challenges to come closer to Him.

᪥

It is a very special honor to have written these accounts for the Gateways Organization, which is a guiding light to countless Jews on their spiritual journeys. I especially want to thank Gateways Founder and Director Rabbi Mordechai Suchard, for giving me the privilege to meet the individuals profiled and to present their compelling stories in this anthology. May Hashem grant him many opportunities to use his considerable talents in awakening Jews to their heritage and strengthening their bond with their Creator.

Debbie Maimon
5769

Foreword

The Gateways Organization, established in 1998, is an educational organization whose mission is to empower Jews of all ages to explore their heritage and the richness of Jewish values. Headquartered in Rockland County, NY, the organization has expanded to 7 vibrant divisions that service all segments of the American-Jewish community.

- **Classic Gateways** sponsors *Family Weekend Retreats*, where families experience uplifting and stimulating Shabbat weekends. In addition, Classic Gateways sponsors weekly classes and home and office study throughout the year.
- **Russian American Jewish Experience** (RAJE) operates from the RAJE Center in Brighton Beach, Brooklyn, sponsoring programs whose goal is to spark Jewish life and ensure continuity for the next generation of Russian American Jews.
- **The Brownstone** attracts collegiates and young professionals across the US to a ten-day immersion in Jewish learning and living, via *Metro Trips* and *Identity Weekend Retreats*.
- **Connections** is a singles networking forum that provides a comfortable place for singles to meet and find a life partner, with a team of matchmakers facilitating introductions.
- **J-Prisms** offers life skills and professional development seminars as well as personal growth workshops, from a Torah perspective.
- **E-Education online** provides personalized answers to questions posed by the Jewish community through **www.AsktheRabbi.org,** as well as virtual classes available for downloading.
- **Celebrations.** Gateways hosts uplifting Pesach, Shavuos, Succos, Selichos and Rosh Hashana retreats for the observant community, infusing these sacred days with inspiration and *chizuk.*

The men and women we encounter in *The Gateways Diaries* bear testimony to the hunger for meaning and faith that inspires "ordinary" people to make unusual sacrifices in their lives. As their private stories spill forth, we cannot fail to be moved by the difficult choices with which they grapple, and the humor and grace that illuminate some of the most trying moments in their respective quests.

May we, too, be inspired to strive for an ever-deepening faith and the courage to make changes *l'shem shomayim.*

Rabbi Mordechai Suchard
Adar 5769

The stories anthologized in this book first appeared in *Yated*. We offer our grateful acknowledgement to the editor, Rabbi Pinchos Lipschutz.

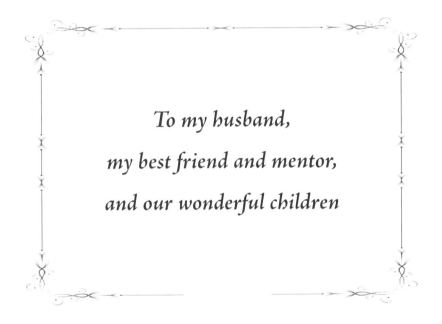

To my husband,
my best friend and mentor,
and our wonderful children

Table
of Contents

Strong in the Broken Places

Steven's Story

I was an American-Jewish college kid backpacking through Europe, eager to see the world. But shortly after I started my trip, I sprained my ankle badly. Instead of touring Paris, I lay on my back in a seedy youth hostel, barely able to hobble to the bathroom.

Sharing the space in the youth hostel were some French guys, cold, stuck-up types who made a pretense of not understanding a word of English whenever I asked for help. Since I spoke no French, we just kind of stared at each other. They didn't want to be bothered with me and left me totally stranded. Without crutches, I couldn't even get to a phone. Without a phone, I couldn't get to a doctor, contact a friend or get something to eat. From being an independent, take-command type of guy, I was suddenly helpless. And so infuriated I wanted to punch someone.

So there I was, incapacitated, furious, hating Europe, especially France, with all my might and wishing I were back home in Plainsville, Idaho. Just two weeks ago, I was desperate to leave that town.

When I was finally able to limp around, I changed my ticket to get back home as soon as possible. An acquaintance from the States who had heard I was laid up dropped in to see me. She said, "Steve, how about doing Israel before you go back home?"

"No thanks, I'm sick of being a foreigner," I told her. "I just want to lie in a hammock back home and vegetate."

"Take my advice and do Israel before you go back home. It's a whole different scene. For one thing, over there, even if you *want* to be ignored, they won't let you. You sprain your ankle, you have a whole crew of people giving you first aid, dragging you to a clinic, giving you advice about what to do today, tomorrow, the rest of your life!"

I laughed. After what I'd just gone through, it sounded appealing. My mental image of Israel at that time was a whole bunch of people wearing khaki pants and sandals and dancing the hora. Folksy and harmless. I felt no personal connection, since being Jewish meant nothing to me. I never even had a bar mitzvah.

Ironically, I ended up going to Israel and staying on a kibbutz for a few months. I picked up some Hebrew in an Ulpan, marveling at the openness and friendliness of Israelis. On weekends, I'd travel around the country, often ending up in Jerusalem. There was a kid from the Bronx I'd met the first week. Everyplace I went—Haifa, Eilat, Jerusalem—I'd bump into this guy.

We finally said hello and got to talking and he told me he was in a summer program at a yeshivah called Aish HaTorah. He invited me to spend weekends in his apartment since it was often half-empty this time of year. He actually gave me the keys to his apartment. This was when I had known him for all of twenty minutes.

So while I was staying at this secular, nonreligious kibbutz, I started coming to Jerusalem for weekends and staying at an Aish HaTorah dormitory. I ended up going to some classes there and getting into the *baal teshuvah* scene and a way of life that was strangely appealing, for all its weirdness.

So there I am in Jerusalem for one Shabbos after another, and I'm getting invited to religious homes for meals with the other Aish HaTorah guys. I'm finding out that Orthodox Judaism is a user-friendly religion. The scene of parents and children together around the Shabbos table really gets to me. I find myself wondering what life would have been like growing up like this.

There was one home where I was invited back many times. The Kriegers were an elderly couple who usually had some of their married children and grandchildren at the Shabbos meal with them. Once, after the meal, Mrs. Krieger, who spoke good English, began talking to me after most of the company had left. We were in the kitchen, and after serving me tea with some cake, she began to tell me a little about her life and her experiences during the Holocaust.

I was mesmerized for two hours. She had survived some horrific experiences and she was full of gratitude to G–d for His goodness to her. She asked me if I'm familiar with the Biblical story of Joseph—how he became Pharaoh's viceroy in Egypt and what his aged father later said to him when they were reunited after a separation of 22 years. "I had no more hope of ever seeing you again," she quoted. "And now G–d has even shown me your children!"

"This is how it is for us," she said. "We never dreamed we would live through the war and have the privilege of coming here to *Eretz Yisrael*. On top of that, Hashem has also blessed us with wonderful sons and daughters and beautiful grandchildren. Such *nachas!*"

I'm listening to her and I'm taking in the whole scene in the little house. I'm thinking that this must be the climax of a long, winding road, a husband and wife facing down the horrors of the past by raising a beautiful, close-knit Jewish family and watching with joy as the next generation comes along. A husband and wife side by side, sharing the ups and downs, growing old together…

I find it hard to leave the tiny apartment, where every time I come, space seems to open up miraculously to accommodate more little grandchildren. Since I'm planning to go back to the States, I don't know if I'll ever return here, so I take a long, slow look around before I finally go.

After a year in Israel, I'm back to America. I quit college for a good business opportunity that came my way and I move to New York where there are lots of religious Jews. There I am, wearing a *kipah* and *tzitzis*, trying to export back to the States the inspiration I picked up in Israel … and I'm trying very, very hard.

But I can't keep it going. I have no address, no network, no place to connect with other Jews like myself. Jewish outreach has not yet made it on the scene. Besides no support system, there is plenty of opposition from family and friends. Like a plane trying to land without the right landing gear, I crash.

Ten years later, I'm marred to Ellen, a girl I knew in high school, and we're living with our two sons in Monmouth, New Jersey. My insurance business is doing very well. We belong to an old-style Conservative synagogue. Like many of the other people there, I go to services Saturday morning and then to work afterward. Our sons are in a Conservative day school.

One day in December, we're eating out in an Italian restaurant. The waiter comes over to take our orders, looks at my four-year old son and says real loud, "So what are you going to ask Santa Claus for?" Right then, there happens to be a lull in the conversation in the restaurant, and the waiter's question comes out with a booming pitch that ricochets across the room. Just about every single person there turns around to hear my son's answer. He pipes up, "We're Jewish. We don't believe in Santa Claus."

Dead silence for a good half a minute. Ellen and I look at each other in shock. He's only four, how does he know this? And how does he know to blurt it out so boldly in front of a roomful of eyeballs staring at him? I'm so proud of him, tears come to my eyes. My wife switches the subject, but later my son goes back to it and asks me, "Why don't we believe in Santa Claus?"

I can't answer him without explaining to him not only what Jews do not believe in, but what they *do* believe in. And since I don't know myself, I can't give my son a real answer.

And that bothers me for the rest of the evening.

Another incident: We're at our nephew's wedding, an interfaith marriage with both a rabbi and a priest presiding, real multicultural style. The priest is an eager-beaver type with a goofy smile. The "rent-a-rabbi" standing alongside him is a gaunt old geezer with loose jowls hanging down in a kind of mournful frown. The priest and the rabbi go through their routines and the wedding rolls along with raucous music and dancing. My wife and I feel sick.

It's three in the morning, and I'm lying awake thinking about the wedding. I try to visualize the future wedding album, with the priest and the rabbi side by side, the goofy smile and the foolish frown. Suddenly a caption pops into my head. Under the priest it says —"We got one!" and under the rabbi, "We lost one!"

A few months later, a niece of ours gets married to a Catholic guy, and my wife and I talk our way out of attending the church ceremony, though we do attend the reception with heavy hearts. This event hits Ellen very hard.

When our son has his bar mitzvah a few months later, we get another wake-up call. His friends fill up almost a whole pew, but it's obvious that from all these boys, not more than one or two is actually Jewish. *Almost all of my son's friends are Christian.* That thought sinks in like a lead weight. In about seven, eight years at this rate, my son might—*might? probably will*—follow in my nephew's footsteps. The priest's goofy smile and the rabbi's mournful frown… *We got one! We lost one!*

This is the turning point for us. We take our younger son out of the Conservative school and enroll him in an Orthodox day school. Then Ellen and I sit down to confront the enormous problem that lies ahead: Neither of us is ready for an Orthodox lifestyle. I'm more ready than my wife, but I'm scared to death of it. Mostly I'm scared to quit working on Saturday, scared my business will take a dive.

Ellen has no interest whatsoever in the outer trappings of Orthodox Judaism. The dietary restrictions seem pointless and keeping Shabbos, a big burden. What's going to happen with our *own* family traditions, she wants to know. Friday nights in our family are for shopping with the kids at the mall; franks and French fries at our favorite eat-out place; TV instead of homework. Throw all that overboard…for what?

I march in with reinforcements. Not only that, but our five-year old is going to be coming home with all kinds of stuff about Shabbos and holidays, stuff we don't keep, I remind her. What's that going to do to him? Soon he's going to be learning not just Bible stories, but Talmud and Jewish law, and that's way out of my league. I won't be able to do homework with him. I won't have a glimmer of what it's all about.

One thing hits us in the face: the need to learn more. At this point, we receive a flyer from the day school about a three-day seminar on Judaism. We're intrigued. The organization sponsoring it is Gateways and the topics address some of our biggest issues. So we pack up to go, but before we get into the car, my wife turns to me and says, "Steve, Torah Judaism is not the answer for me. I just know, deep in my gut."

"Do you want to cancel this whole thing?" I ask her.

"We won't know a soul there."

"Are you saying you want to cancel? Just tell me."

"No, but I just want you to remember when you get all swept up in this, that I had a premonition we were headed for trouble."

Ellen's Story

I was right. We certainly were headed for trouble. But it didn't happen all at once. That first seminar was really wonderful, once we got over the awkwardness of sitting at a Shabbos table, not knowing a thing about any of the rituals, even *Kiddush*. We found the lectures fascinating. They gave the Torah perspective on everything from raising children and marriage to science, archeology and history. And none of it seemed threatening. At least, not at first.

What happened was that the seminar awakened this old romance

Steve had with Orthodox Judaism when he was younger. We went back home after the weekend and got back into our old routines—well, I did anyway. But Steve was interested in the follow-up programs Gateways was offering. There were classes, learning partners, tutorials, a whole network of outreach activities. Steve was brimming with enthusiasm, just like a kid discovering Disney World.

All of a sudden it wasn't just the philosophical interest in the religion—which I shared with him—that was turning him on. It was the down-to-earth, practical dimension like Shabbos and *kashrus* and other laws that he wanted to get into. I was scared he would want to go the whole nine yards, something we had agreed we weren't ready for.

To make a long story short, there were some very difficult moments over the next year as we fought over how much religious practice to incorporate into our lives. How much I could tolerate, versus how much Steve could bear to do without.

Truthfully, what kept the issue from escalating into a full-blown crisis was our growing connection with Gateways. To begin with, the frequency of the seminars lightened the tension of what do about Shabbos and holidays. Since making Shabbos for ourselves at home wasn't working, we accepted Shabbos invitations from religious families we met through Gateways. But soon I'd had enough of that, and Steve did, too. We were starting to feel like gypsies.

The Gateways weekend and holiday seminars were a wonderful solution. Keeping Shabbos there was painless—actually pleasurable. Sitting around the Shabbos table, we made new friends and had some marvelous conversations with people going through the same religious "mid-life crisis." We became close to one of the rabbis and his family. And the lectures opened up volumes to us. It was exhilarating to be there.

The children's program was a hit with my kids. The striking thing about it is that the kids kept Shabbos there, too, without any complaints. But it was a tumultuous time for us. The closer we came to Jewish observance, the more distant our friends and family became. When we started keeping kosher, we thought our friends would go the extra mile and choose kosher places to eat out with us. But it didn't happen that way. They dropped us. We felt isolated, in limbo, not feeling part of any community. And Steve and I were still not on the same page, so that made the loneliness worse.

Things came to a head when Steve went too far. I was finally dealing with Shabbos and keeping kosher, but Steve wouldn't let it go at that. He got this idea into his head that his insurance business wasn't up to Jewish ethical standards—it wasn't honest enough—and he wanted to phase it out, just when he was finally making it and we were beginning to reach a level of financial comfort.

He told me about his decision on a Friday, right before we were supposed to set off for a Gateways seminar. All Shabbos long I was holding myself in, biting back words like, "You're being irresponsible, fanatic, crazy!"—the very words that had been thrown at us by intolerant family members ever since we began our journey back to observant Judaism.

I rehearsed the speech I would make to Steve when we had some privacy, to let him know how I wasn't prepared to stand by and let him destroy whatever we had. That speech never did get delivered. Shabbos afternoon, I went to a class given by Mrs. Reich on the "secret of Jewish femininity." The lecture had been offered at previous seminars but I always skipped it. For some reason, I decided to attend.

The "secret" had to do with the spiritual dimension of the husband-wife relationship in Judaism that lies at the core of true intimacy, and the wife's innate ability to nurture it. It touched a deep chord in me. Somewhere during that hour, my pent-up anger at Steve evaporated. I began to see where his stubbornness was coming from. He was trying to juggle some totally incompatible values and he didn't want the choices he made in this "juggling act" to ever make him ashamed.

If I got my way, it's very likely those choices *would* bring him shame. Was that the role I wanted to play? The wife who persuades her husband to violate his conscience? Was that the route to spiritual union in a marriage?

The class was over. I left, blinking back tears. Something had crystallized. I could finally see a direction. I knew that even if hard times still lay ahead, Steve and I would tough it out. We'd get to the finish line, G–d willing. A little battle-scarred perhaps, but as Hemingway put it, "Life breaks people. But afterwards, people are strong in the broken places...."

ஃ

Today, Steve and Ellen are one of the prominent couples in a small nucleus of religious families in a town near Lakewood and are known for their hospitality—especially to people on the "journey" to Jewish knowledge. They recently celebrated the birth of a baby girl. When the baby was just a few weeks old, they flew with the family to Israel for Pesach. When he visited the Kriegers with Ellen, the elderly couple was beside themselves with happiness to see him. "We never dreamed we'd see you again," they exclaimed, "and here Hashem has also showed us your wife and children!"

The Longest U-Turn

Sara's Story

Jeff and I got married while we were still in college. We experimented together with eastern religions and New Age ideas. Finally, we embraced Christianity. Our conversion was bitterly received by our families, and we distanced ourselves from them even more by moving out west to Wyoming. With the exception of Brad, Jeff's older brother, our families gave up on us.

Jeff had a bit of money and we bought a ranch. I worked as a copywriter and he enrolled in computer courses.

But Brad refused to turn away from his kid brother. He had recently become observant himself and couldn't accept that Jeff had abandoned Judaism. Brad kept up a steady email correspondence with Jeff, and sent him a series of tapes by Rabbi Tovia Singer, who lectures to audiences across the United States about missionaries and cults.

Jeff listened to them halfheartedly, hoping to find ammunition to back up his own theological arguments with Brad. But the tapes had an unexpected effect on Jeff. I was shocked when Jeff admitted that he was beginning to have doubts about the truth of Christianity. I was terrified that Jeff might actually forsake the Church. When he told me he intended to attend a Gateways seminar that winter, I tried to talk him out of it. And when that didn't work, I made up my mind to go along with him.

Confrontation is not my style, but desperation made me bold. I planned to seize every possible opportunity to show the rabbis the truth of the Gospels. For me, everything was at stake—my marriage, my religion, my whole life.

Something astounding happened during that weekend. In one lecture, the very verses I had planned to quote in support of my Christian beliefs were presented as examples of deliberate mistranslations in the Christian Bible! The speaker compared what he called the true meaning of the words with their "false" meaning as taught by Christian

Scripture.

I sized up the rabbi as a slick talker who knew how to twist the truth. But it didn't make sense. Why would he lie about something so easy to check out? Any Hebrew-English dictionary would expose him. As I listened, I started to sweat. What if he's right? I ran out of the lecture room, too upset to speak. What if everything I believed about Christianity was based on fraud? Who could I trust in this world of lies? "G–d, show me the truth!" I sobbed.

Trust was a major issue in my life. I was orphaned as a child and grew up in different foster homes. Some were better than others, but I learned early in life not to trust people. Those who seemed to care usually had ulterior motives, and they didn't keep you for long when you no longer served their purposes. In college, I met some young missionaries who were genuinely kind. I gravitated to them and converted to Christianity. I needed to believe in a powerful Someone I could trust.

And now I was in the midst of people dedicated to uprooting the faith that had come to mean so much to me. I felt more threatened by Judaism than by anything I had ever experienced. I couldn't hide my turmoil. Some of the rabbis tried to help. They gave me hours of their time, helping me through what was turning into a major religious and identity crisis.

Jeff and I were poles apart about everything. He was very excited about his re-discovery of Judaism. He wanted to throw everything overboard and move back east. I was against such a drastic move, and we had some intense arguments. But my biggest problem was the guilt and fear that plagued me for even contemplating leaving my church.

You have to understand the terrifying role the devil plays in Christianity. For Christians, the devil is as powerful as G–d and no human being can overcome him alone. Absolute faith in the Christian "savior" is the only defense against this evil power: anything that challenges that faith is the result of the devil's machinations.

I began to realize that what was keeping me bound to Christianity wasn't faith in the "savior" as much as an immobilizing fear of the devil.

At Gateways, the rabbis took away the terror. It didn't happen overnight; it took several months. Rabbi Suchard, Rabbi Rietti and others showed me endless patience. One of the things I learned that affected me profoundly was that Judaism perceives the devil—*the soton*—as a force that is only as strong as a person allows it to be, and that the *soton's* true purpose is to bring out a person's deepest strengths. Every person can defeat the *soton* through his or her own *mitzvos*.

For people lucky enough to have had a Jewish education, that might be nothing new. For me it was the most liberating insight in the world.

One afternoon, I was coming off a u-turn on a highway and found myself at the base of a steep incline. I was driving upwards, straight into a magnificent sunset. Buildings, skyline, and roadway all fell from view. The heavens surrounded me on all sides in magnificent peach, pink and lavender hues. The beauty of it was blinding. Tears came to my eyes as the truth hit me with great force: No higher evil power existed or could ever exist. There is only Hashem. He had opened my shackles. I was truly free.

Jeff's Story

I was born Jewish and I attended a Conservative Hebrew School for close to twelve years. In my twenties, I felt a spiritual vacuum. For a while, I explored other religions and eventually joined a church. In another drastic step away from Judaism, Sara and I became born-again, Evangelical Christians, and we were quickly recruited to proselytize Jews. Missionary work is an obsession of right-wing Christians.

My family was deeply disturbed by my conversion, and relations between us deteriorated. I had always been close to my brother, Brad, and he refused to give up on me. He had become a religious Jew in the last few years. The tapes he sent me by Rabbi Singer confused me. I confided my doubts to my wife who was very shaken by my admission that I no longer felt secure in my beliefs.

I was driven to find out the truth even if it meant finding out that I'd made a disastrous mistake by becoming a Christian. I flew to New York to meet Rabbi Singer. We had long talks and he urged me to attend an upcoming Gateways seminar.

Rabbi Singer and the Gateways seminar changed the course of my life. I learned about the permanence of the Torah. I learned about the source for the Jews' refusal to change even a single letter of it, from the earliest centuries till the present day. In contrast, over 400 versions of the Gospels have been written in English and other languages, and they're constantly being revised. I myself had seen many Gospel versions. No two are exactly the same and they contradict each other, but they all claim to be the Divine truth!

The rabbis pointed out one example after another in the Torah where G–d makes a covenant with the Jews and promises it will be forever, such as with Shabbos and circumcision. Yet the entire Christian Bible is founded on a denial of those promises. The Gospels preach that the laws of the Torah are no longer necessary; all that counts is having faith in the "savior."

I was advised to study the Written Law in the original Hebrew, not from a Bible translation. I had enough Hebrew background to do that. I discovered how the authors of the New Testament had altered and deleted material in many places to make the Scriptures conform to Christian theology. The evidence of fraud was a real bombshell to me.

At Gateways, the rabbis stayed up with me till the early hours of the morning, working through all my questions. They sent me tapes of other classes when I went back to Wyoming; they gave me encouragement over the phone. Eventually, I found myself on the threshold of leaving the Church, but even at that point, it was almost impossible to take that step. The emotional seduction of Christianity is hard to resist.

A Christian is not supposed to question or challenge. The catechisms cloud your reasoning, your ability to think. On some level, you sense that it doesn't add up, but the fear of being a heretic and going to hell is overwhelming.

My marriage was extremely shaky at this point. Sara was convinced that by returning to Judaism I was forfeiting my soul. The Gateways rabbis were urging me to move to a Jewish community where I wouldn't be alone. I prayed to G–d for wisdom and for the courage to do what was right. I didn't know if I had the strength to make the break with Christianity.

Today I know that a Jew who takes the first step toward Torah is blessed with tremendous help from Above. My brother Brad, Rabbi Singer, Gateways – they were all part of Hashem's intervention in my life. Without His help and His special messengers, who knows where I'd be today?

Where, in fact, are Jeff (Shlomo) and Sara today, ten years later? They are members of a religious Jewish community, where Shlomo works in electronics while keeping up a regular learning schedule. Sara just finished writing her first screenplay.

Their two sons are a source of great nachas *to them. Yehudah will celebrate his bar mitzvah next spring, G–d willing. Nachman is five.*

"They're both so compassionate," Sara marvels. Each, in his own way, will notice a child in the room who is feeling lonely and become his friend."

She's grateful for the Torah environment that embraces their children. Sara recalls how Nachman got an early taste of Torah learning. "Shlomo would bring him to the beis medrash when he was just an infant and rock him in his infant seat while he learned there. Until he was two years old, Nachman spent three hours each morning soaking up the sounds of Torah. He absorbed that holiness each day. It's no wonder he has such a special neshamah!"

Bring
Us Close

Ben's Story

I had just finished college and had started working at my dad's pharmaceutical company in Lawrence, New York, when I met Shana. She was nineteen at the time; I was twenty-three. We hit it off right away, although the difference in our religious backgrounds was something of an issue. Shana comes from a very religious family and went to Jewish schools all her life. I'm Jewish but grew up without any exposure to a Jewish lifestyle.

Shana had gradually moved away from her family's style of practicing Judaism. She still kept kosher and wouldn't drive or work on Shabbos, but many of her activities crossed the boundaries of her previously sheltered existence. She loved her parents and didn't want to hurt them. So she led a kind of double life, doing things one way at home and another when she was at college or with her friends.

She didn't tell her parents about me, even when we had become serious about each other, because she said it would upset them too deeply. They had hopes of her marrying an ultra-religious yeshiva student.

Shana was conflicted about many things in the religious world. She'd had her share of run-ins with authority figures in the schools she'd attended and some of those confrontations still rankled. She said people in her community didn't understand or respect her. They wanted her to dress more conservatively and have higher religious standards. Ironically, I found her to be a very religious person. It was obvious that she had a deep respect for Judaism.

One example: I was telling her about a buddy of mine, describing him as a brilliant, funny, life-of-the-party type—an all-around great guy. "That is, except for one little fault," I admitted. "He's got a stingy streak."

Shana wasn't impressed by the superlatives. She told me the rabbis who wrote the Talmud said that a person's true nature is exposed by three types of behavior: his dealings with money, how quickly he gets angry, and how he behaves when under the influence of alcohol. She explained the wordplay in Hebrew, *kiso, kaaso and koso*, that refers to these character traits.

"This buddy of yours might be fun to be with," she pressed her point, "but if it cost him money, could you count on him in a pinch?"

The question rankled. "Of course I could count on him!" I said. "He'd be the first to offer a hand."

But suddenly I wasn't so sure.

I was intrigued that some rabbis who lived three thousand years ago, centuries before Erikson, Freud or Jung, had come up with such astute insights into human nature.

The encounter with the "rabbis" didn't end there. After we started seeing each other seriously, Shana asked me if I would be willing to learn about the basics of Judaism. My ignorance in this area was so pronounced, it bothered her. She felt I would never be able to understand her without knowing more about the Jewish faith and why her close friends were all Jews.

Most of these friends came from religious homes, although not all of them observed Judaism as their families did. It often happened that someone would make a reference to an upcoming holiday or a Jewish ritual I never heard of, or tell a Jewish-style joke that went over my head. It made me look kind of dumb.

I grew up in the mid-West till I was in my teens without any clue that there were any laws in Judaism other than to be a decent, ethical person. In fact, I remember a line my mom used to say, "You know what I love about being Jewish? It's so easy—no obligations!"

Actually, there *was* one obligation when it came to me. I had to learn to read Hebrew in order to perform at my bar-mitzvah. So I was sent to Hebrew school twice a week starting at age eleven. I was in a class with a bunch of kids who, like myself, were bored out of their wits and saw no reason to be there. We did nothing in class but throw spitballs at each other and pull pranks on the teachers. Miraculously, I did learn how to read Hebrew, but only on a primitive level.

Shana wanted me to understand how she envisioned her future home. It involved a lot more than knowing how to read Hebrew and knowing the names of the holidays, she said. But it wasn't something she was capable of explaining to me, herself. She asked if I'd be willing to attend a weekend seminar on the basics of Judaism. I had no interest in sitting through a bunch of lectures and said so.

"It would mean a lot to me. If you really don't like it, you're free to leave," she said.

"I already don't like it, so why go in the first place? I can't imagine any intelligent person believing in the Old Testament—"

"Judaism is bigger than the Old Testament."

"But isn't that the starting point?"

"You're thinking it's just Bible stories—"

"It'll be like warmed-over Hebrew school that I hated sitting through as a kid."

"If it is, just walk out."

"Okay, I will."

"Just do me one favor, Ben. Go with an open mind. And remember, I've been a rebel since high school. I hate having things forced down my throat. So I would never do that to anyone else. Especially you."

So that is how I ended up at a Gateways seminar. I walked in there looking as cool and un-Jewish as I could. Unshaved, tight leather motorcycle jacket and threadbare jeans, big bandana across my forehead, dark sunglasses … earrings… I knew it was tasteless to come that way to a religious event on the Sabbath, but it was easier for me to have people write me off as a weirdo so they wouldn't bother with me. No one would care when I walked out.

So there I was, Friday night, in a ballroom with about four hundred people, just finishing up the Sabbath meal, which happened to be superb. There were some nice people at my table and I was starting to chill out when someone announced a list of classes planned for the evening. None of them interested me and I was starting to edge toward the door when this young-looking rabbi came over to me and introduced himself as Rabbi Kohl.

He made some small talk and asked if any of the classes on the program appealed to me. I shrugged and said I hadn't decided yet. On an impulse, I asked if he was giving any of the lectures. He said he would be speaking about how to raise sane children in today's world.

"…by raising them religious," I finished the sentence for him. He took the teasing good-naturedly. "No religious dogma tonight, scout's honor," he said, punching me lightly on the shoulder. "I'll be looking for you."

He found me later on in the lobby. Instead of going to his class, I'd been catching up on the sports section of the New York Times. *Better not start up with me*, I warned him in my head. *I'll give you a real run for your money.*

Apparently, he wasn't too worried. He sat down next to me and we started chatting. I could see he was wondering what brought me to this seminar when I obviously had no interest in being there. But he didn't ask. We talked a bit about the news, politics, that kind of stuff. After a while we moved to one of the side rooms where it was less noisy.

Suddenly, my questions came spilling out from different directions, surprising me as much as the rabbi.

I wanted to know how Christianity and Judaism were different. I wanted to know what Judaism teaches about free will and determinism, about the purpose of suffering. What was the purpose of keeping kosher in the twenty-first century? What sense did all the Shabbos restrictions make? How did Judaism reconcile with evolution?

Looking back, I was demanding a entire seminar from this rabbi in a single sitting. He could have said, "Look, you'll find many of the answers you're looking for if you attend the classes here. Isn't that what you came for?"

He could have said that but he didn't. He sat there patiently with me as I fired away. Soon we were swept up into a discussion that went on for hours. He knew all the weak spots in Darwinism. Obviously he had studied the subject well. He kept going back to the concept that everything in creation cried out against the theory of randomness.

I couldn't argue with that. Since studying the extraordinary properties of DNA in biology classes, I could no longer see the world as haphazard. There was too much perfection and symmetry in nature. We went through a lot of the other issues I brought up, and then he kind of drew me out about myself.

I started telling him about what was going on in my life; my relationship with Shana and how frustrating it was for us that although Shana had finally told her parents about us, they refused to even meet me. They refused to accept that we were deeply serious about wanting to get married. They were still trying to set her up in the traditional matchmaking way with ultra-religious guys in black hats.

Rabbi Kohl heard me out. He explained that the religious path is so sacred to Torah Jews that seeing one's children forsake it—even a part of it—is felt as a tragedy. Parents feel they're losing not only their children but their grandchildren and great-grandchildren. "It's a wound that never heals," he said.

When we finally wrapped up our marathon that Friday night, I felt that I'd met someone I could trust. It was way past midnight and we were both exhausted. I don't know what was going on in Rabbi Kohl's head. Probably he was dying to just stagger into bed. So was I but I had a phonecall to make first. I took out my cell phone and then stopped short. *Shabbos*. "Well, so what?" I thought. But I shoved it back into my pocket. It wouldn't kill me to wait till the morning. I'd make up my mind what to do then.

To make a long story short, Gateways created a major upheaval in my life. For one thing, it started me on a quest that I had never intended to undertake. Unexpectedly, it created problems for me, too, in my relationship with Shana.

Once I decided I wanted to live more Jewishly, I understood that it was not simply a matter of keeping a few restrictions. I needed an education. With the help of Rabbi Kohl, I made plans to go to Israel and spend a few months in a yeshiva for beginners. Shana, who had urged me so strongly to learn about Judaism, wasn't happy about this turn of events. She worried that I'd come back too religious for her. She worried what the separation would do to our relationship. She actually had misgivings about having sent me to Gateways!

One thing we did agree on is that we would get engaged before I left. We were elated when Shana's parents finally agreed to meet me. I had put on a *kipah* but the meeting was a shock for all three of us. Shana's father was an older man with a gray beard. He embraced me kind of clumsily, looking as if he were about to cry. Her mother looked like she hadn't slept in a week but managed a wobbly smile. I wanted to reassure them that everything would turn out all right but I too had gnawing doubts.

Could I ever infiltrate this complicated religious world where despite my age and college degree, I knew less than any five year old?

❧

Ben went to Israel in May. He enrolled in a beginner's program in a yeshiva in Yerushalayim, staying on until right before the yomim noraim. Despite initial difficulty settling in, it was a time of significant growth. Three weeks before the wedding, Ben flew back to the States. He and Shana came together to the Gateways Rosh Hashana seminar.

Ben remembers the sensation he felt standing in shul on what he called "the first Rosh Hashana of my life":

The rabbi was making the *bracha* on *tekias shofar*. I couldn't help remembering how when I was a kid, all of this was meaningless to me. I used any pretext to worm my way out of having to go to temple. Prayers, sermons, *shofar*-blowing—none of it touched me.

Now, so many years later, I found myself almost trembling in anticipation of the *shofar's* call...*A time of Divine favor...Hashem is opening His arms to you. Ask Him for whatever you need.*

What did I need most? Once, my biggest problem in life was how to get Shana's parents to give us their blessing. Amazingly, they had done so. But now it was Shana who wasn't happy. I had come back from Israel different. I was too serious, she said, too much into being a *baal teshuva*. What a crazy twist! Once, she had begged me to go to a Gateways seminar to develop an appreciation for Judaism. Then, *I* was the one resisting. Now I was back here, praying for the same turnaround in her heart that she had prayed for in mine. Could life get any stranger?

I stood there feeling troubled and confused. The cry of the shofar split the air. It was so piercing, it drowned out every thought in my head but one. "*Please Hashem, bring me close to You* with Shana!" I prayed over and over, tears streaming down my face. That's all I was able to ask for. I knew if He granted me that, I'd have everything.

Ben and Shana were married a few weeks after Rosh Hashana. Pictures of the wedding show a radiant choson *and* kallah *amid joyous family members and friends. The couple settled in Far Rockaway, where Ben works as a pharmaceutical assistant. He keeps up his learning with the help of two* chavrusas *affiliated with a local* kiruv *organization. Shana is working on a graduate degree in nutrition. In the interview for this story, Ben expressed his and his wife's deep appreciation to Gateways and to Rabbi and Mrs. Kohl for their devoted friendship.*

What
I Owe
Him

Elizabeth's Story

My first encounter with G–d came when my son, Joey, became seriously ill at the age of five. The doctors suspected leukemia. The diagnosis would be confirmed if certain symptoms got worse. Dread came in waves as I imagined I saw my little boy getting weaker, imagined I saw the shadows under his eyes turning darker, his skin becoming jaundiced. I was terrified. I felt like I was going to crack.

I had always believed in a Higher Power, a force far removed from my daily life. But the idea of a G–d who might care about what I was going through was foreign to me. If there was a G–d who could save my son, I was ready to do *anything* to win His help. I was ready to give my life for my little boy. For the first time in my life, I began to dwell on the thought that perhaps G–d wanted something from me, other than to be a good person. But what could He possibly want from me?

With only a vague notion of prayer, I turned to G–d in desperation. I put my son's life in His hands. I begged Him to save Joey. I made a conscious decision that if my son recovered, I would give him the opportunity I never had myself for a Jewish education. I made all kinds of deals with Him, and I meant them with all my heart. I prayed over and over, "Please save our child, G–d. Give me a chance to raise him as a Jew."

My Joey passed the crisis point and slowly began to recover. It turned out that he had a serious infection, not leukemia as we had dreaded. I felt from the deepest place inside me that G–d had answered me and it was now up to me to fulfill my part. As part of my promise, we enrolled our son in the Shalom Torah Academy, an Orthodox day school.

My husband Michael and I began taking our first steps in learning about Judaism. We became involved in several outreach programs, particularly the Jewish Learning Center in Monmouth County. On one occasion, we were asked to host a *melaveh malkah* in our home for the members of the program.

It was a fateful occasion for us. The rabbi who spoke that evening recounted moving stories about the extreme dedication of Jews in different parts of the world at different times in history. Hearing about these people who made some of the hardest sacrifices in life for the sake of their faith, we felt proud to be Jews.

Afterwards, as a token of thanks for hosting the *melaveh malkah*, Michael and I were offered a gift certificate for two to a Gateway weekend retreat. We happily accepted.

I remember some of the classes vividly. Rabbi Suchard showed one example after another of major prophecies from the Torah affecting the Jewish people and world events that had materialized throughout the centuries up to the present day. Each one defied logic and the laws of nature but nevertheless came true.

"For those of you with any degree of familiarity with the New Testament, have you ever wondered why no prophecies appear in that book when the Torah is replete with prophecy?" he asked.

"The answer is obvious," the rabbi said. "Both books present themselves as the word of G–d. But making prophecies in G–d's name is a risky business. Unless you're omniscient and in complete control of history—in other words, unless you're G–d—making promises about the future is going out on a dangerous limb. If you're not G–d, and you're foolish enough to pretend you are, a failed prophecy about world events could fatally undermine your credibility. It's not the kind of mistake a person trying to spread a new religion could afford to make."

That was pretty thought-provoking. I caught Michael's eye. I could see he was itching to check this prophecy thing out. I was pretty sure he wouldn't find any King James Bibles in our hotel drawers, though, to satisfy his curiosity about the rabbi's claim. The cross-checking would have to wait.

Even more amazing than this argument was the realization that I had believed in the Torah without knowing it! All my life I ascribed to certain New Age principles that I thought were in contradiction to Judaism, like the concept of the soul traveling through time and having more than one life. At Gateways, I began to discover that this, too, is part of Torah, that the Torah is the source for the spiritual truths to which I gravitated.

Since that first Gateways experience, Michael and I have been to three more, including one on Yom Kippur. The passionate prayer of these Jews on Yom Kippur was almost from another world. I've never heard or seen anything like it.

About six months after that first seminar, we *kashered* our kitchen. Shabbos was a bigger hurdle, as we kept taking two steps forward and one step backward. But it's becoming less difficult with time.

For me, the hardest part in becoming religious is trying to keep harmony at home. Michael and I have been moving at very different paces in our observance. In the beginning, when I saw I couldn't count on his support, I was very disappointed. He would poke fun at my "obsession" with religion and I would criticize him for being intolerant.

Our marriage, which had been pretty solid, began to suffer from the impact of this discord. Michael felt it was my fault: I had introduced something alien into the relationship and expected him to accommodate me he when he wasn't ready to. I had to admit he was right. I was being torn apart. Wanting to be closer to G–d through the Torah conflicted with the harmony and love in my marriage.

Not only that, almost every relationship within my family presented a separate hurdle. The underlying message was "You're changing so much we no longer recognize you! We have nothing more in common!" When I could see beyond their opposition to their fear of losing me, I became much less defensive. I was able to reassure people that I was really the same person inside. But often that realization was only in hindsight, after a draining emotional scene and much pain and tears.

It took Michael a long time to acknowledge that I'd made a commitment and intended to keep it. My heart knew that Joey was alive and well because G–d had answered a frantic mother's prayers. How could I back out of my promise to raise this child Jewish? How could we raise him Jewish if we ourselves were not practicing Jews?

Gradually Michael became more accepting. But then a major glitch arose: I discovered the laws of family purity. My learning partner arranged by Gateways taught me the laws, and I took a tour of a *mikveh*. I had a deep desire to experience this *mitzvah*, but Michael was adamantly opposed.

I remember us sitting together during breakfast Sunday morning at a Gateways seminar and I was getting ready to go to the next class. It was on "Jewish Women in Marriage." Michael sighed and half-joked, half-grumbled to someone sitting next to him, "This is the class that causes all the trouble, the one on family purity. I don't know why women go for it. No man in his right mind would."

"How do you know?" I challenged him. "Maybe religious husbands appreciate it."

"I doubt it. They're religious, so they have to obey. I'm sure if it were up to them, they'd chuck it in a minute."

"Why don't you ask? There's Rabbi Suchard right there. Ask him."

"Watch out. I just might."

"Why don't you? Go right ahead and ask him what Jewish men get out of the family purity laws. Ask if they're a major hindrance to happiness."

To my amazement, Michael turned around and caught Rabbi Suchard's eye.

"Rabbi, can I ask you something?"

Rabbi Suchard stopped at our table. "Sure."

Michael pulled out a chair for him, saying, "I just need a minute, if you don't mind." The rabbi sat down. I hastily excused myself and hurried out of the dining room. I was dying to hear what the rabbi would tell him, but I knew it would be better if they talked man-to-man. I never did get a full account of that conversation. But it was enough for me that when the subject of *taharas hamishpachah* came up again, Michael was much more understanding. Wonder of wonders, he was ready to give it a try.

To understand what this *mitzvah* means to me you have to visualize my lifestyle. I live in an upscale neighborhood in New Jersey. My hair hangs loose, I wear jeans, we go to movies, have social obligations with non-Jewish friends. There's no way I can be a really complete Jew right now. For many reasons, I'm not ready to overhaul my life yet.

The only time and place I can be a complete Jewish woman is when I go to the *mikveh*. There, it's just me, my inner Jewish self and my connection with Hashem. After the blessing, I say a prayer in my heart. I ask Him to help me find a way to make my faith stronger, to be able to keep the *mitzvos*—and never to lose sight of what I owe Him.

How Green
My Valley

Jeanette's Story

Chutzpah runs in my family, along with a weird kind of idealism. My father's father was a teenage revolutionary in the years leading up to the Russian Revolution. The czar was hunting down revolutionaries with a vengeance and my grandfather was desperate to leave the country. With the help of a relative who was an officer in the English Parliament, he smuggled himself out of Russia into England.

It was a stunning escape, but his odyssey was far from over. England had no use for Communist revolutionaries, especially Jewish ones. The relative in Parliament had to find a nice way to get rid of my grandfather before they both got into trouble. At the time, England was pushing for a Jewish homeland in the spirit of the Balfour Declaration. The relative decided to ship the young Commie to what was then Palestine.

My grandfather landed in Haifa and joined the nearest kibbutz. What happened to this man whose revolutionary fervor was his whole life? He found a perfect outlet for it with Jabotinsky, a charismatic Zionist leader who was dedicated to the founding of a Jewish socialist state in Palestine. Like many Jews of that period, my grandfather was one of those walking paradoxes: deeply Jewish and proudly committed to creating a utopian haven for the Jewish people, yet claiming to be an atheist. He raised his son—my father—the same way.

My dad grew up on an anti-religious Hashomer Hatza'ir kibbutz. He never stepped inside a synagogue or saw the inside of a Torah until he was in his late twenties. As a young man, he left Israel and settled in America, where he married my mother, a second-generation American with even less Jewish background than he had.

Despite this, my home had a distinctly Jewish/Sabra tone to it. We picked up Hebrew from my father and celebrated Jewish holidays; though he made a point of letting us kids know the holidays were purely cultural celebrations, like July 4th and Thanksgiving. I had my bat mitzvah, like all my Jewish friends, in a Reform temple.

I went the collegiate route and ended up at Rutgers University with a Jewish clique of close friends. A number of us found jobs in Washington afterward. I always wanted to do something bold; politics seemed to offer me that opportunity. Working for Senator Charles Schumer as a legislative assistant—one of his "Jew-crew" as we called ourselves—I felt I could make a difference. That illusion petered out after a while, but the job opened my eyes to many truths about people, power, and politics.

One of our group who landed a terrific job as a news writer for *The New York Times* began taking an interest in learning more about Judaism. Someone steered him to an ultra-Orthodox retreat one summer at a place called Torah Institute in Moodus, Connecticut. That in itself was bizarre because Michael was a brilliant freethinker who hated authoritarianism. He was actually a little like how I imagined my grandfather, the revolutionary.

Michael should have taken one look at Orthodox Judaism and grabbed the next bus back home. When he told us after the summer that he had decided to quit his job to study at a yeshivah in Jerusalem, we were flabbergasted. We thought Michael had fallen in with cultists, except he didn't look like a zombie. He sounded exactly like himself. But we couldn't take him seriously because his new opinions upheld things he had ridiculed all his life.

Although he'd look us up when he came back for vacations to the States, most of the gang dropped him. He'd call up old friends and try to get together, but we weren't interested. He was religious now, with a *kipah* and dark clothes, and his politics were all the way to the right. We simply had nothing in common anymore.

I almost forgot about him but there was this *Shanah Tovah* card from him stuck in a pile of papers on my desk. For some reason, when I trashed piles of junk mail and stuff I didn't need, it wasn't thrown out.

On an impulse, I sat down and wrote to him a two-line note:

"Skip the theology, Michael, and tell me one thing: How does a brilliant, independent mind who couldn't tolerate authoritarianism swallow Orthodox Judaism?"

He responded in the same kind of "shorthand," scribbled on a postcard.

"I'll tell you. When it's a bunch of clowns telling me how to live, they can go jump in a lake. When it's G–d, that's another story."

"How do you know it's G–d?" I wrote back.

"They proved it to me and I can prove it to you. But you have to be ready for it," he challenged me.

We began corresponding. Our letters were filled with theological and philosophical debate. But it all came to an abrupt halt when Michael left the beginner's yeshivah he was studying at and transferred to one that was more advanced. He let me know why I wouldn't be hearing from him. For someone who wanted to focus totally on his religious studies, he said, it wasn't "appropriate" for him to be corresponding with me. I was stunned. I walked around for days feeling deflated and empty. Clearly, he had become fanatic.

But he had started something percolating inside me. He really believed that G–d had spoken directly to the Jewish people thousands of years ago and that all of the Torah's laws were immutable. After much vacillating, I followed up on Michael's challenge to learn more on my own about Judaism.

The first Gateways Seminar I attended took me by surprise. I had expected a lot of preaching and blind-faith fundamentalism. But I didn't hear any of that. The speakers spent time establishing the Divine origin of the Torah. They argued that morality and ethics are meaningless unless they're G—d-given. If values are arbitrary, then one man's saint is another man's villain and absolute good and evil don't exist.

Besides the actual content of the lectures, the rabbis with their families were fascinating to watch. The kids were all dressed up on Shabbat; they sang along with their parents at the table. Something about them was so captivating. The lectures focused on ideology; the kids brought Judaism to life.

Here's how I felt at the end of that weekend: like someone with a piece of costume jewelry who discovers after many years that the jewels in it are real. And here she's been throwing this thing around, treating it like a cheap trinket!

Some real heavy issues came up in my life in the weeks and months after the Gateways event. With the help of some friends I'd met through Gateways, I had begun to keep kosher and I was learning about Shabbat. These changes brought me into conflict with my parents, especially my father. I couldn't bring up the subject of Judaism in my house without having him drag out all kinds of stale jokes and put-downs. The humor started to wear thin and we had some sharp arguments. I'm tough – but my dad's tougher. My mother was caught in the middle. I realized it was time for me to move out.

On a visit to Israel that summer, I stayed with my grandparents in Tel Aviv and traveled into Jerusalem to find some people Gateways urged me to meet. Shuttling between the Tel Aviv scene and Yerushalayim did something peculiar to me. I couldn't stomach the beach-and-disco scene after being in Jerusalem. I began to toy with the idea of taking off a year to study in Israel. But I got an urgent message from America that one of the positions I'd interviewed for before going to Israel had called back. They wanted to hire me. That changed everything.

It was a dream-come-true job. I was hired as one of the producers for a popular celebrity show. The pay was excellent, the work fascinating. I felt like I'd finally "arrived." For a while, I was so consumed with this new job, I put everything else on hold.

One day I heard from one of the rabbis from Gateways about an upcoming seminar. He suggested I get my parents to come with me to this one. The idea was so outrageous I had to laugh.

Strangely enough, my parents actually agreed to come. My father made it clear he had his own agenda. What he really wanted out of this event was to challenge the rabbis in an all-out debate—something I dreaded having to watch. I've never met anyone yet who could score the winning point in an argument with my father.

He came to the seminar with his boxing mitts on and I watched tensely from the sidelines. All Shabbat long I waited for the explosion, for the confrontation my father was sure to engineer. But it never came.

I still don't know what it was exactly that took the wind out of his sails. But something happened to him. At one point before the Shabbat services, Rabbi Suchard offered to show whoever was interested in going up to the Torah for an *aliyah*, how to make the *brachot*. My father kind of snorted and looked at my mother. She shrugged. Slowly but deliberately, he stepped forward. For the first time in my life, I heard him make a *brachah*. I couldn't believe my ears. His Hebrew is flawless, but he stumbled a little bit over the words. My eyes stung. Now I knew that miracles really do happen.

By the end of the seminar, I had reached a decision to quit my job and go to Neve Yerushalayim to study. I knew I would face terrific opposition from my parents. I dreaded telling them, because I didn't yet have the words to explain why I had to do this.

"Jeanette, this is insane," my father exploded when I told them. "Do you know how many people would give their most valuable possession for the job you're throwing away?"

"Doesn't your career mean a thing to you?" my mother chimed

in. "How can you be so irresponsible?"

I knew exactly how they felt because my friends and I had read the same riot act to Michael when he ditched his job to learn in a yeshivah, and we weren't even his parents.

I said, "Mom, Dad, this is something I have to do. Before I throw myself into the rat race out there, I have to find out what's in my own backyard."

"I'll tell you what's in it," my father thundered. "A rut! A hole! You want to be stuck in a rut all your life? You could be sitting on top of the mountain and you're going to throw that away? For what?"

I had asked myself that question, too. I had an answer, but it would have sounded childish to my parents, so I kept quiet.

I had already glimpsed the summit of my father's mountain. It only looked exalted from a distance. From close up, it was empty, disappointing. I was drawn to the verdant valley—the "rut"—my father so disdained, with its promise of richness and fertility.

"Where will it get me?" I answered them in my heart. "To a place I need to get to, a place a Jew is meant to go."

The Sign Said: Keep Out!

Tracy's story

Three months away from our wedding day, Jeremy and I still hadn't found a rabbi who was willing to marry us. It was maddening. We'd call and make the appointment and the secretary was always so nice and friendly. Then we'd come to speak to the rabbi and feel the atmosphere freeze as soon as we walked in the door.

The conversation always took the same turn. "Why do you want an Orthodox wedding?" the rabbi would ask, taking in Jeremy's uncovered head and my own nonreligious attire. "What do you know about the format of a religious ceremony? Are you aware of how utterly different it is from a Conservative or Reform affair?"

Maybe it wasn't logical, but Jeremy and I had this thing about being married Orthodox, even though we weren't Orthodox ourselves. Jeremy comes from a traditional family; they keep kosher at home and observe the holidays. One of his brothers became religious and goes to a yeshivah. My background is Conservative, but as a Sunday School teacher, I know a lot more about Judaism than the rest of my family. I wanted a different kind of wedding than what I was used to in my social circle, something more serious, more Jewish. We both felt that the Orthodox way was more authentic.

But every Orthodox rabbi turned us down. The fourth one we went to said he couldn't help us unless we intended to keep Shabbos and something called the laws of family purity. He told us to go home and think it over and he gave us a few books to read.

So we left. By that time we were so discouraged we didn't even look at the books. Without much discussion, we said okay, we'll do Shabbos and family purity, whatever that is. I thought, why make such a big deal? Jeremy and I knew about not driving and using electricity on Shabbos; it wouldn't kill us to try it. How difficult could "family purity" be?

So we returned to Rabbi G. and told him we agreed to his terms. To our surprise, he didn't look at all happy. In fact, he looked downright upset. He had a paperweight on his desk, a glass square with a globe of the world inside, and he took it in his hands and kept turning it around and around, saying nothing.

Finally, he looked up.

"Look, Tracy, I'll be very honest with you," he said. "I checked into the information you gave me the last time you were here. I can't do the wedding for another reason. It is highly doubtful that you are Jewish."

I was shocked speechless. I turned to Jeremy. His reaction mirrored mine.

"How can that be?" he finally managed. "Everything Tracy told you is a hundred percent true. She's been Jewish since the age of twelve. Are you saying you couldn't confirm that?"

"According to my information, her conversion took place under the auspices of a Conservative rabbinic court. Such conversions are not valid according to Jewish law."

"But my father told me it was," I stammered. My heart was pounding. I felt like I had just been told I had a serious disease. "He said the rabbi assured him that they followed procedures that would make the conversion valid to everyone, even the Orthodox."

"The rabbi who told him that was misinformed. I'm sorry. I know this comes as a blow to you. You can check with another rabbi if you wish. But I must tell you, I doubt that any Orthodox rabbi will recognize your conversion."

I was afraid I would start crying if I said another word. Jeremy asked why I couldn't just do the conversion again, the Orthodox way.

Rabbi G. answered it was not so simple. "Becoming Jewish involves far more than a few token procedures," he said. It was an all-encompassing transformation of identity that could only take place within the framework of whole-hearted commitment to uphold the laws of the Torah. He said the Jewish religion does not seek converts and that living an observant Jewish life is far more daunting than we realize.

He asked us if we had read the books he gave us. Jeremy said "No, not yet."

Rabbi G. turned to me and said, "Discussing conversion at this point is premature. No Orthodox rabbi will perform a conversion for someone who is not committed to keeping the *mitzvos*. It doesn't matter how deeply you want to convert, or how Jewish you may already feel. Until you know what Shabbos is, what *kashrus* involves, what it means to be surrounded by *mitzvos* every waking moment, an emotional attraction to Judaism is meaningless. When you've read the literature I gave you, come back and we'll talk."

He started to say something conciliatory, but I got up and stumbled blindly out of the office. I was furious at this rabbi for discrediting my Jewishness. We were the biggest fools for trying to find an Orthodox rabbi to marry us.

The irony was that I was the person in my family with the most Jewish pride, and the most Jewish education! I had been teaching Sunday School for three years and loved it. I spoke Hebrew, had been to Israel and yearned to go back. Jewish history was one of my favorite subjects. I felt Jewish in every bone of my body. How could Rabbi G. dismiss all this as "meaningless"? I was wounded to the core.

I had converted twelve years earlier when my father remarried a few years after my mother's death. My Jewish stepmother had requested the conversion, as I had not been raised Jewish, even though my father and my grandparents were Jewish. I was actually eager to convert, since I was very close to my grandparents and they encouraged it.

Whatever religious tension existed in my life during my adolescence came from being more meticulous than my parents about keeping Jewish holidays and traditions. In college, I majored in Judaic studies and moved in Jewish circles. There was never any doubt in my mind that I would marry Jewish and have a traditional Jewish home.

Until this moment.

Jeremy caught up to me and tried to talk to me but I was too distraught. Something inside me had shattered. Even though I didn't follow Orthodox practice, I knew good and well that their traditions were older and more rooted than any other branch of Judaism. I didn't want to be Jewish only according to Conservative or Reform Judaism. That was like having your MRI read by a paramedic instead of a radiologist. Even if he gave you a clean bill of health, how secure would you feel?

But I didn't want to accept Rabbi G.'s conditions and start from the beginning like a child. I just couldn't bring myself to do that. And it wasn't as though he had offered me a shred of encouragement. I felt like there was a sign on his door saying, *Keep Out*. His message between the lines to me was, "You think you want to join this club? We're going to make the requirements so hard, you're going to think twice!"

Dad was furious. "What kind of a nerve does this guy have?" he yelled. "You're not Jewish enough for him? Tell him if he needs proof, I've got it! Tell him I have the receipts from all the tuition I paid for years of Hebrew School for you; I have the receipts from all the money I paid for your bat mitzvah! That ought to be good enough proof for him!"

Jeremy and I were torn. I sensed that he was as troubled as I was by the doubts Rabbi G. had raised about my conversion. The thought that his children might not be considered Jewish was as devastating to him as it was to me—especially since he had been moving closer to religious observance.

In the end, to please him, I decided to attend a Jewish outreach event—a Gateways seminar that a friend of mine recommended. It was supposed to explain many of the essentials of religious observance. Despite my hurt and anger, I really wanted to understand where Orthodox Jews were coming from, and why they were so quick to reject anyone outside their turf. I also hoped I would be able to find someone who would hear my case, someone easier to deal with than Rabbi G.

I walked in feeling pretty hostile. Instead of a nametag, I felt like wearing a sign: *Conservative and Proud of It!* I felt like a coiled spring. Jeremy kept telling me to chill out; there was no point in slamming these people. They were not to blame.

I calmed down over the weekend because it was hard not to respond to the friendliness and warmth from just about everyone. The speakers were incredibly knowledgeable. In spite of my resistance, I found the classes enlightening, and I felt the wall of ice starting to melt. The class on Jewish marriage moved me deeply. Who wouldn't want a marriage like that? Another lecture that presented proofs of the Divine origin of the Torah made me take a second look at what I was taught to view as "rabbinic Judaism"—laws the rabbis allegedly tried to "sneak" into the Torah.

Conservative and Reform Judaism have a lot of issues with the Orthodox over this peeve. But at the seminar, one of the speakers, Rabbi Rietti, took apart this claim. He detailed the history of some of those "rabbinic" laws, showing how they were always part and parcel of Jewish observance.

He expressed the idea that the Torah doesn't sanction the modernizing of Judaism because Judaism is not an art: it's a science. "Imagine a construction worker building a bridge," he said. "If, purely for aesthetic reasons, he decides to deviate from the blueprint, how long will that bridge hold up? The Torah is G–d's blueprint for building a bridge in this world that will take you to the next one, the World Of Truth. Getting from one side to the other is risky business and many people don't make it. The rabbis who know how to read that blueprint know that to alter it can be disastrous."

He described the meticulous safeguards that throughout the ages protected the Torah from tampering and human error. A Torah scroll with even one letter purposely altered loses all its sanctity, he told us. It can't be used any more and must be disposed of. If not for the stringencies of these laws, mistakes and other changes would have crept in and after many centuries, there would be thousands of variant editions of the Torah. No one could be sure anymore that his Torah was really the "word of G–d."

It was fascinating to contemplate the fact that all Torahs, from every part of the world, are identical, and have been so right down through the centuries. And this was before computer spell checks! I began to understand why Orthodox Jews are so protective of their traditions.

During that weekend, Jeremy and I witnessed something else that truly inspired us: a *"Hachnosas Sefer Torah"* ceremony. We watched the finishing strokes being written on the Torah parchment in a hushed room. I saw the awe on people's face and the tears it brought to some eyes. I thought about what I had just learned about the history of those letters. They were G–d-given; they were holy, unalterable.

Rabbi Suchard captured the emotion in the room. "The ink of the last letters on the Torah is drying," he said, "but our tears are still wet. The impact of this event will remain long in our hearts." He spoke of how fitting it was to celebrate the completion of a new Torah in a place dedicated to bringing Jews back to their spiritual roots. And what an honor for the Torah to be used for occasions that inspire Jews to reconnect with its teachings. No matter how distant a Jew may be, the Torah is still his home and he can always come back to it.

I felt that he was talking directly to Jeremy and me. He was saying, "Come home, you can do it. We'll help you." I knew I couldn't go back to Rabbi G. I felt too humiliated over the way my true background had been discovered and how I had broken down in his office. But there were rabbis here who I was sure would help me do what I needed to do to become Jewish according to *halachah*.

I knew there would be hurdles; I knew it wouldn't be easy. My parents, his parents, our friends, our jobs… Suddenly everything seemed upside down. We had come to Gateways thinking our biggest problem was finding an Orthodox rabbi to marry us. Now we knew that the real challenge was not the rabbi or the wedding. It's what comes afterward—making a truly Jewish home.

❧

Tracy and Jeremy met people from the Gateways staff at a Manhattan event about three months later. No one recognized Tracy at first. "We remembered her as a girl with long, blondish hair who looked kind of unhappy," one person remarked. "And here was this young woman with covered hair, a long skirt, and looking radiant! Then we saw Jeremy and it clicked. We were thrilled for them. There were hugs and 'Mazal tovs' all around."

Tracy reported that she had quit her job at the Sunday School because she got the distinct impression that her new look and ideas were regarded as subversive. "I don't want to be challenged at every turn about Orthodox Judaism because I'm not yet equipped to explain or defend it," she said. "Jeremy and I still have so much to learn."

Strangers
at the Gate

Frances' Story

My father was a hardworking plumber; he and my mother started out with very modest means. Then some lucky investments on the stock market launched them into sudden wealth. They joined the circle of *nouveau riche* Jews in the wealthy suburb of Norwalk, Connecticut. I was their only child, raised as a classic Jewish American Princess—pink phone, pink rug, more clothes than I knew what to do with. My first car was an Audi.

I got everything I wanted, but I was never happy. My folks wanted me to go to a private school because it offered a superior secular education compared to the public schools in our area. I was sent to a quasi-religious Jewish day school where some of the staff was observant, but none of the students were from religious homes. My parents didn't reckon that their daughter would come home with religious notions about Shabbos and G–d and Torah. They would humor me by listening to me recite what I'd learned in school, but they attached no importance to it. They made it clear they did not want religion to encroach on their lifestyle.

Our home was luxurious, but a cold place. I fought with my parents constantly, especially in my teen years. My father's parents lived nearby and when I felt the need to escape, I'd run to my grandparents. I loved the Jewish flavor of their home. Grandma would light Shabbos candles Friday night and my grandfather sang Shabbos songs at the table. There was a special aura in their home that stole into my heart.

My grandfather made his living as a butcher. People respected him for his high ethical standards in business. He was a gentle, loving person, and very serious about his religious routines: he went to *minyan* every morning. I remember rehearsing my bat mitzvah ceremony in front of him, reveling in the tears of pride I saw in his eyes.

My grandparents never called me Frances. To them, I was Feigeleh, their beloved only grandchild. I wanted our home to resemble theirs, right down to the old-fashioned, time-worn, cherry wood furniture. I would pester my parents, "Why can't we have a *mezuzah* on our door like Grandma and Grandpa? Why can't we have Shabbos like they do?" They'd brush me off impatiently. "Frances, we're not Grandma and Grandpa. They live their lives; we live ours!"

When my grandparents died within a few months of each other, I was still in my teens. To this day, I feel I never properly mourned them, never gave vent to the aching loss I felt. I turned my back on the precious gift they had given me—a love for the Jewish way of life. I was too young to understand its worth. When I was nineteen, confused and rebellious, I decided to marry my non-Jewish boyfriend.

My parents were mortified. What would their rich Jewish friends think? They threw every argument they could think of to talk me out of the marriage. They even invoked the memory of my grandparents... how I'd be hurting them and their legacy by marrying out of the faith. I thought bitterly of how as a child I had begged my parents to keep Shabbos as in my grandparents' home. Why couldn't Grandma and Grandpa's wishes have mattered to my parents as much in life as they did in death?

My marriage was an unhappy one and ended in a painful divorce after just a few years. When it was over, I was so emotionally exhausted all I wanted was to raise my two sons in peace.

A memory from those early years after the divorce stands out sharply. I had taken my older son Mark to the orthodontist. It was a long appointment, and with time to kill, I decided to take a walk around the neighborhood. I strolled a bit until I found myself in front of a building with a sign on the front that said Beth Hillel Day School. I wandered inside.

Walking through the halls gave me an intense sensation of *déja vu*. The floor tiles, the two-tone blue walls, the bulletin boards, all triggered memories of my childhood. I stopped at a bulletin board and read the children's compositions.

Second Grade - Mrs. Levine: "When Moshiach Comes"
Sixth Grade - Mrs. Wengrov: "Courage Is…?"
Fourth Grade - Mrs. Kaufman: "What Chanukah Means To Me"

Suddenly, my throat ached and tears rolled down my cheeks. I stood there for several minutes trying to compose myself. A woman approached me and asked me if I was a parent in the school. When I shook my head, she said, "I'm sorry, but I have to ask you to leave." A camera posted inconspicuously above eye level had reported my presence to the office staff. "Please understand," she said apologetically. "It's nothing personal, it's a school rule. Only those who have identified themselves at the office are permitted in the halls."

I nodded and hurried out.

Years passed. I moved with my children again, this time to Tom's River, ten miles from Lakewood, New Jersey. I found Lakewood a strange town, inhabited by rabbinic looking men and their families. People said these men led severe lives; they said they were intolerant and overbearing, that their religion oppresses women. But I watched the fathers clasp their little children's hands as they crossed the street. I saw them standing on line in stores, overheard fragments of their conversation with their kids and their wives. They carried groceries, carried children, pushed strollers. They seemed caring and attentive. Was it all just a show?

Once, walking around the lake with my younger son, I tentatively approached one of those bearded men. "Excuse me, are you a rabbi? Can I ask you…I have a few questions about Judaism…" He nodded. I blurted out a question, sounding semi-incoherent to my own ears, but the man didn't seem to notice. "Do you have something to write with?" he asked me, as though it were an everyday occurrence to be approached by strangers asking philosophical questions about Judaism. He gave me a telephone number, explaining that this person gave classes to beginners in Judaism.

It sounded so easy. Just make a phone call. Come to a class. Learn a bit. Meet some new people. What could be simpler? But I didn't do it. Fear of making major changes in my life stopped me. "Courage is being willing to change," a sixth grader at Beth Hillel Day School had written. How could she be so wise at the age of eleven? Sadly, I didn't have that kind of courage.

About four years later, I had remarried – this time, to a Jew— and my oldest son was thirteen years old. I took my children on a drive through Lakewood one winter evening. "Let's walk a bit," I suggested. I parked the car and we strolled down the block. Chanukah menorahs burned brightly in the windows, tiny orbs of golden light shimmering in the darkness. We counted as many as three or four menorahs in some of the windows. We paused in front of one house, taking in the scene. A family stood in a semicircle as the father guided a little boy's hand that held a lit candle toward the menorah. The wick caught the flame, the child beamed, mother and father exchanged radiant smiles. They all clasped hands and began to sing.

I looked into my sons' eyes and read the wistfulness there. How they would love to be part of a scene like this, I thought sadly. We have a membership in a special "club" but we can't use it. We can't even get in the door! Are we destined forever to be strangers looking in?

I wept silently as we walked back to the car. A decision hardened in me that night. I went home and searched my drawer. It took hours, but I found it: I clutched the piece of paper I'd been given so many years ago at the lake. I dialed the number.

The person at the other end heard me out and put me in touch with a Rabbi Danziger. He, in turn, steered to me to Rabbi Ezriel Munk who invited me to his Torah classes for beginners. My husband was wary, but supportive, and I took the fateful first step.

I began learning about some of the fundamentals of Judaism through the weekly Torah portion. The astounding message of Jewish history began to fill me with pride. Despite so much suffering and calamity, the Jews remained a vibrant, growing, spiritual people. I could relate to that on a personal level: I had seen the bitterness and suffering life could bring, yet I longed for spiritual clarity. The saga of my people gave me hope.

As time went on, I knew I had found what I was looking for and I shared it with my family. Rabbi and Mrs. Munk became our mentors, the people in my Torah classes our new circle of friends. The Lakewood families we met in connection with the classes were wonderful. They never tired of having us visit. "Come for Shabbos," they urged, "Come for Purim!" "Come for Yom Tov!"

Only a few weeks after I started learning, my husband and I attended our first Gateways Seminar. The classes were intriguing: "What are the Hidden Lessons in the Ten Commandments?" "Why Pray?" There was a class on "Sages, Saints, and Charlatans" that opened my eyes to how Torah wisdom ennobles a person. There were classes for women only, about relationships from a Torah vantage point, about tolerance, growth, and compassion in a marriage. Above all, there was warmth and camaraderie there that touched my heart. We were all Jews trying to catch up on lost time, fellow travelers on a common quest.

Now, two years later, thinking of all the turns my life has taken and where I am today, I recall a child's book I used to love. The book had a picture of a salmon on the front cover. His name was Red Tag because scientists attached a tag to his fin so they could track him. The story follows this little fish as he lives out the majority of his life span in the ocean. Then, in his final months, Red Tag sets out for the place where he was born, an exhausting journey of thousands of miles.

Months later, he reaches the site. He tries to leap upstream, over the rapids that separate him from the lake where he was spawned and to where he must return. Totally spent, he can't make it over. Yet instinct keeps driving him onward. Suddenly, he makes one giant, last-ditch effort. The image of him leaping frantically into the air still stirs my emotions, 25 years later. This time he succeeds! He's finally home. Now he can rest, create the next generation of salmon, and live out his remaining days…

So here I am, swimming my own thousand-mile journey upstream…back to my grandparents' home. It was there that a little girl's heart was nurtured with the faith of her people. It's been a long and crazy saga getting to this point. But the wondrous thing is that the obstacles I was so sure would turn me back just sort of melted away.

All along, I thought the gate to that exclusive Jewish "club" was locked, but I found out it only looks that way from the outside. Once I gave a tiny push, the gate opened wide. There never was a lock at all.

A
Heartbeat
Away

The haunting melody evoked the strains of *Chasidishe zemiros* and the homey warmth of the *shtetl*. Surprisingly, the impromptu singer at this Gateways *melaveh malkah* was a thirtyish-looking man with long hair, jeans and a tattoo on the back of his right hand holding the microphone.

It was Hal Gottesman, who was attending the Gateways Shabbaton with his wife, Randy. He worked as the manager of a music store in upstate New York and Randy was a fashion designer. They appeared to be assimilated American Jews with little or no Jewish background.

But that image dissolved as Hal sang on. The emotional resonance in his singing coupled with some of his mannerisms—eyes tightly closed, the slight *shuckling*, the way his right fist punctuated the air as he sang—were strong giveaways. This was a young man who had almost certainly been raised in a religious home, who had spent countless hours around his family's Shabbos table.

There were more than a hundred nonreligious participants at the *melaveh malkah* and they were fascinated by his performance, applauding enthusiastically when he finished. Hal smiled but seemed bewildered. The long odyssey that had led him to this moment was peculiar, to say the least.

Hal (Chaim) had grown up in Williamsburg, one of several children in a Chasidic family. His elderly father was a Holocaust survivor. When the Nazis invaded Hungary, Hal's father was in his forties and the father of a large family. The Nazis deported and murdered over a hundred members of the Gottesman clan. No one came back from the camps except for Hal's father. When he was liberated from Auschwitz, he was a frail, broken man. Hal was born in America about eighteen years later.

Hal had an older brother, Moshe Aharon, who was developmentally delayed. The older boy's disability made him the butt of ridicule in yeshiva from a clique of boys as well as from some of the *rebbes*. Hal shared his brother's rage and anguish. Like many children of Holocaust survivors, the boys felt they could not involve their parents in their problems. They tried to deal with their tormentors in their own inept way, which compounded their social isolation. The experience produced the seeds of rebellion in Hal that slowly turned him away from the lifestyle and community in which he had been raised.

Hal was able to pinpoint the event that finalized his abandonment of the religious community:

I was in my teens, in Israel, where I was learning in a yeshivah. One day, one of the boys told a couple of us that he knew where we could get a video and watch it. I knew I was doing something forbidden and could be kicked out permanently for it, but I took the chance. That decision sealed my fate. After watching that video, and later other films, and reading some books, I felt like I had crossed over to a place of no-return. I couldn't go back to living an innocent life, even if I wanted to. And I didn't want to. One thing led to another until I was officially out of yeshiva and on my own, no longer religious.

My father was not a man of many words. He tried to reason with me. He and my mother insisted I come home, but I wasn't ready to do that. I was over the threshold for good. They cut me off, refusing to send me any money, and I had no means of support. I stopped calling them. For two years, I roamed about Israel, living with one friend or another, doing odd jobs.

Fifteen years went by before Hal saw his parents again. In that time, he moved from Israel to England and to Puerto Rico, before returning to America and moving in with friends in Queens. Years of drifting had made him sick of living without direction. He went to college and learned computer programming. By the time he met Randy, he thought he finally had it together: a job that had growth possibility, a place to live that was more than temporary shelter, and good friends. The only thing he lacked was a bridge back to his family.

Randy saw that she could fill that role:

After I took Hal to meet my parents, I said, "Okay, now it's time for me to meet yours." Hal swallowed hard. I knew they hadn't seen each other for years and years, and barely spoke in all that time. Hal was longing to see them again, though he wouldn't admit it. He was just a heartbeat away from making that phone call. He was afraid of being rejected, of starting the whole cycle of pain and anger all over again. There was a lot of guilt, too.

We talked about it and he finally called them. I think the phone wires must have been smoldering from Queens to Williamsburg from all the emotion on both sides. Hal told them we were getting married and asked if they wanted to see him and meet me. They only thing they asked about me was, "Is she Jewish?"

When we finally all met, it was a pretty heavy scene. Everybody cried, including me. There was something so sad about it. Here were these kind, gentle people, and here was their son, who was more like them than they could possibly know. Why did 15 years have to pass before they could hug each other again? Hal's father had lost so many people he loved due to war and hatred – and then almost lost Hal through nothing more than the craziness of adolescence.

I had never in my life spoken to anyone Chasidic. To me, Hal's parents were totally foreign, but his mother won me over right away. It was almost uncanny. Say you landed on Mars and found yourself talking to Martians. And you discovered that they like children and apple pie. You'd say, "Hey, we're not so different after all." That's how I felt.

After the first meeting with Hal's parents, there were long discussions about how to compromise on a wedding where both sides of the family would feel comfortable. Ultimately, their conclusion was that it was impossible. So Hal and Randy had two weddings! They got married with *chupah* and *kiddushin* in Williamsburg, where Randy wore a *sheitel* and a gown that met Williamsburg standards. "It was an incredible experience," she says. "I loved every minute of it." After that, they were "married" again at a gala wedding in New Hampshire, where

Randy's family lives.

Shortly after Hal's reconciliation with his family, he was introduced to a rabbi in Monsey with whom he developed a close connection. Hal slowly began to explore Jewish learning. The rabbi encouraged them to attend a Gateways seminar, promising that it would be an enjoyable and memorable experience.

For Hal, Gateways opened a door to a room that was both familiar and strange. "I had never heard anyone argue the truth of Torah using logic and history and archeology," he admits. "I had to kind of turn off the old tape playing in my head to hear this new one. Suddenly, I was processing all this fascinating information about Judaism that went totally over my head when I was a teenager."

At the *melaveh malkah*, the band was playing some traditional *nigunim*. Someone noticed Hal humming along and offered him the mike. After a moment's hesitation, he took it, jumped onto the stage, and began to sing. At first, it felt as though he was play-acting. Gradually, those forgotten melodies began to work a certain magic on him. Feelings he had not had for many years began to stream. And then—*A dam inside me broke! I wasn't doing an impersonation of someone singing. It was really me. The words, the melody—everything came flooding back.*

For the first time in fifteen years, I felt it was possible to come back "home." The warmth in the room, the respect I felt from people ... even though I haven't been religious for so many years. Suddenly, I was wishing my father could see me. He might not have understood the scene here; how could I sing these nigunim and still be the way I am? But I think it would have given him nachas all the same.

The experience led Hal to reflect on his father for the first time from an adult perspective:
My father's suffered all his life. I think he's a lamed-vovnik, one of those secret tzaddikim. He constantly collects tzedakah for poor people and distributes food. He's a gentle, quiet person.

I realized that I never really knew what he was thinking. You can sit at the same table with him for hours and not hear him say more than a few words. There's a lot he can't or won't talk about with me. After all, in terms of the way he'd like me to be, I'm the "wayward son." After so many years apart, we're trying to get to know each other, but it's hard. It's like—you can love someone but still feel like you're strangers. I guess it'll take a while. At least we've come this far.

My Mother Never Told Me

Karen's Story

Do you believe in dreams? Are you the kind that smirks or smiles indulgently when someone tells you that her mother or father, who died years ago, came in a dream with an important message?

I was a skeptic myself. But that was a long time ago, before some strange episodes that turned my life upside down.

My mother died when I was fifteen. A few years after her death, I found out something shocking about her from my sister: Mom had revealed to her that she was Jewish, as were both of her parents. She told my sister that she converted to Catholicism as a young woman, in order to marry our father. One of the rules my parents established at the time was to limit their contact with my mother's side of the family.

We were raised as religious, church-going Christians who went through all the Catholic rites of passage. I never met either one of my maternal grandparents. I was never even shown a picture of them. My father's side of the family was so large that I never felt the lack of extended family on my mother' side. Whenever I asked about her parents and family, I was told that they lived in Australia, that they had never been close.

I was about eighteen when my sister told me this. For almost a week, I was in a state of shock, not wanting to believe it. I became obsessed with trying to find out about this Jewish family, but I was intimidated by my sister's comments that the family had disowned my mom when she converted. Why would they want to have anything to do with her daughter?

I didn't even know at the time that Judaism is passed down from the mother, and that my siblings and I were fully Jewish. Discovering this threw me into another tailspin. I went to the priest and confessed. He told me not to be concerned, that what counted was what's in a person's heart, and that if I accepted the Christian savior, I was a member of

G–d's flock like anyone else.

But certain things began to trouble me. One of them was the Christian view of Jews, portraying them as living in darkness, in sin—as lost souls that need salvation.

I grew up in Tom's River, right on the outskirts of Lakewood, New Jersey, and stayed there after college. I worked as a home-health practitioner and was frequently in Jewish homes. Jews were a large part of my agency's clientele. I got to know them in a family environment where you really see someone up close.

To see them as living in "darkness and in sin"... well, that took an immense stretch of the imagination. They did not look like lost souls in the least. They did not look in need of salvation. They were decent, warmhearted people, with close-knit families and clean, straightforward ways. I liked being around them. I liked driving slowly through Lakewood on a Saturday. Everyone was out walking—families with little kids, husbands and wives, little boys dressed like little men. Where in America do you see such a thing? You could feel the togetherness, the sense of purpose in their lives.

The question began to gnaw at me: What am I, a Christian or a Jew? Which is the right way? But I couldn't even decide who to ask for help with this dilemma. A priest would say, be a Christian. A rabbi would say, you're a Jew. Some even believed you could be both. Where was the truth?

It was around then that I dreamed about my mother. I couldn't see her face but her voice was unmistakable. She said to me softly and with sadness, "Karen, you're a Jew. I never told you, so you couldn't have known. But now that you know, you have to learn what it means."

I woke up crying, not understanding why I felt such sadness. My mother had died six years earlier, and I no longer felt the degree of bereavement one feels when the loss is fresh. The strange thing was that

I also felt deeply consoled. I had received an answer from my mother who—wherever she was—was surely beyond human prejudice. Up to that point, I can't say that I believed in an afterlife even though heaven and hell are fundamental to Catholic dogma. The dream was so powerful, I couldn't dismiss it.

I also dreamed a couple of times about my grandfather, my mother's father whom I'd never met or spoken to and who had been dead for almost twenty years. In the dreams, he was always sitting in the corner of a room I didn't recognize, looking outside into the night, his face reflected in the window pane. It was a face I didn't know. For the most part, he was silent. Once he said a few words in a whisper. I couldn't make out their meaning.

I became preoccupied with these dreams and thoughts throughout the day. It was a struggle to concentrate on my work. Then another weird thing happened. I was working with a client in Lakewood. My eye caught an article in a magazine called *American-Jewish Times* about a lecture being held at the local Jewish Learning Center. The topic was *The Soul and the Afterlife in Judaism*. The lecture was part of a series being offered by a noted lecturer, Rabbi Mordecai Becher, in the Monmouth County Library, about 30 minutes away.

I knew I would be at that lecture if they held it on the moon.

My encounter with *The Soul and the Afterlife in Judaism* at the JLC was the beginning of a very tumultuous period in my life where doors started opening and closing with breathtaking speed. I left the Church behind forever. Judaism had a magnetic pull for me. I went to the library and checked out a half dozen books. I began reading about Jewish history, philosophy and culture.

One day, I took one of the books I had been studying with me to work, to read during my breaks. My client was a religious woman in Lakewood recovering from surgery. Her husband, a rabbi, glanced at the book and asked in surprise, "Are you interested in Judaism?"

I told him I had recently discovered my mother was Jewish and wanted to learn as much as I could about my new-found religion. He took another look at the book and snorted, "This won't teach you a thing. If you really want to find out about Judaism, I'll give you something to read."

He went to his library and came out with a book. "Read this and you'll have an idea of what authentic Judaism is about," he told me. The book was called, *Sing You Righteous* by a Rabbi Avigdor Miller. At my first free minute that day, I took a look inside it.

The book spoke of G-d with the name Hashem, and said He could be discovered through the day-to-day wonders and the wisdom He planted in nature. It was written with deep emotion. It explained Divine Providence, stressing how important it was for a person to deepen his faith by making himself aware of Hashem's guiding Hand in his day-to-day life.

Something happened a few days later that made those words jump right off the page. At one of the classes at the JLC, where I had become a regular, they gave out a brochure for a Gateways Seminar to be held at the end of December. Rabbi Veshnefsky, the director of the JLC, and Rabbi Becher urged me to attend. At this point, I was already eating only kosher and was wrestling with some of the difficult changes this forced me to incorporate in my life. The rabbis felt the seminar would give depth and perspective to everything I had learned until now about Judaism. "You'll see the many bits and pieces merge into a whole," they promised.

I glanced at the dates of the seminar and an eerie feeling came over me. It would take place just when my family had scheduled a vacation cruise. The arrangements for the cruise had been made two months earlier, but for no rational reason, I had cancelled several weeks ago. My family was upset with me, and not having any legitimate reason for being a party pooper, I felt like a fool.

Until I saw the dates: December 23-26, the same dates the cruise had been called for. Was it a coincidence that I had left those days free of commitments? Is this what was meant by Hashem's guiding Hand?

The Gateways weekend was a wonderful experience. It seemed to lift people right out of their day-to-day world into a different kind of universe. It was a place where novices like me sat side by side with people who knew a whole lot more, but it didn't matter. You felt you belonged. There was a bonding among people over the four days we spent together that made me proud to be Jewish.

The atmosphere encouraged people to open up. You felt you were willing to risk exposure. If you mentioned that your grandfather was coming to you in dreams and urging you to find out the purpose of your existence, no one smirked and no one rolled his eyes. In fact, when I spoke about it to one of the rabbis, relating some of my grandfather's messages to me, he seemed genuinely moved. "What a rare blessing that a grandfather is given the privilege to visit his descendants from the world of Truth," he said to me. "And how fortunate for his soul that you heard his message and are returning to your heritage."

After the seminar, I knew I would make two major changes in my life. One: I would seek out my Jewish relatives, no matter how scary that would be for me. Two: I would become Shabbos observant.

I was advised by the rabbis at Gateways who kept in touch with me on a regular basis after the seminar, not to plunge into a religious lifestyle in one massive leap. But I couldn't hold myself back. I knew becoming Sabbath observant could get me fired from my job, but I felt I had to do it anyway. I discussed with one of the rabbis what I would say. I pushed everything off until the end of the week, and then—to my bitter disappointment in myself—I just lost my nerve.

I agonized over what to do all Friday night. Shabbos morning, I woke up with a sense of dread. But a miraculous thing happened. A heavy snowstorm had blanketed the city during the night, and my agency, along with most other businesses, remained closed for the day. "G–d, I thought, You knew I needed a week's reprieve to gather my courage. Thank You."

The following week I asked my two bosses for a meeting. I came right out with it, expecting them to give me the ax immediately. But they were more baffled than angry.

"You were Catholic all your life, and overnight you're becoming a Jew?"

"I was a Jew all my life, but I didn't know it," I said. "I found out about my mother only recently."

"Your father's a Catholic, isn't he? That makes you only half-Jewish."

"In Judaism, having a Jewish mother makes you a complete Jew."

"That's only according to the Jews. Catholics are not bound by that."

"Well, being a Jew by birth, I *am* bound by it."

"Look, you can choose to be a Jew and still live a normal life, can't you? It's not like you'll be excommunicated if you come in on Saturday. I mean, most Jews I know have no problem…"

"I'm doing this out of conviction. I think I can make it worthwhile for you to keep me on, even without the Saturdays, and that's what I'd like to discuss."

In the end, they kept me on, with obvious ambivalence. I think they felt the Jewish thing must be temporary insanity, and that I'd drop it after a while. In the meanwhile I felt elated that I had "come out of the closet" about my Jewishness. "Mom, I'm doing this for you, too," I said in my heart. "I know this will bring you peace."

Here's a truly amazing example of the kindness of the Lakewood religious community: When I began to keep Shabbos, the word spread among some of my Jewish clients. For many weeks after that, until I moved to Lakewood and was able to accept invitations for meals, every Friday afternoon I would receive a package containing everything a person could possibly need for Shabbos. Candle-lighting times and explanations for important rules about Shabbos would accompany the traditional foods. Friendly instructions such as "Now relax; time for a Shabbos nap," were slipped inside. What a community, this little town of Lakewood!

In the following weeks, I traced my mother's Jewish relatives. There was a whole clan of them. Some lived in Australia, some in England. I mustered up my nerve and dialed my mother's older sister. I stumbled through an introduction: "Aunt Sylvia? This is your niece, Karen Ashberry, Deborah's daughter..." and waited in silence until comprehension dawned on the other side. Those first few seconds of anticipating hostile rejection or chilly indifference were agonizing.

But then a flood of happiness streamed over the wire. My aunt greeted me with such warmth I choked up, unable to continue. After a while, I was able to loosen up a bit and talk normally. In a rush, it all came out: how my mother had died three years before and that I had only recently discovered I was Jewish and how much I wanted to get to know them. My aunt urged me to visit as soon as possible.

"Karen, send us pictures. That way, when you come to visit, we'll be old friends already," Aunt Sylvia suggested, before saying good-bye.

They sent me pictures of some of the family. My hands trembled as I held the photograph of my grandfather. He was so like what I had expected! The rabbi's words came back to me as the photograph blurred with my tears. "...And how fortunate for his soul that you heard his message *and are returning to your heritage."*

If only I could have met my grandparents during their lifetimes! I try to imagine their heartbreak at being cut off from their daughter... how much it would have meant to them to be able to glimpse the "epilogue" to that sad story. If only they could have known about me, their granddaughter, and how Hashem helped me to discover who I really am and to rejoin the family I never knew was mine.

A Diamond is Forever

There was a glamorous aura of youthful success and affluence about them. He was a senior partner in a prestigious law firm; she had worked her way up to an associate editorship of a women's magazine. They lived with their two young children, Zachary and Jennifer, in a 14-room apartment in an upscale part of Manhattan. Lori joked about being a workaholic, but it was becoming less and less of a joke as she struggled to balance the competing demands of career, marriage and parenthood.

David and Lori were planning to spend Presidents Day weekend in the Bahamas, but four-year old Zachary's asthma attack threw those plans awry. At 9:00 Thursday morning, instead of boarding a plane, they were in the emergency room with their son, with no prospects of catching another flight that day or the next. Surveying the options, David called a colleague at work who had tried to interest him in a Jewish outreach seminar scheduled for Presidents Day weekend. He asked the friend if they could still make reservations. When he told Lori about the idea, she groaned, "Count me out."

"Hey, it's better than staying home," he told her. "They have babysitters for the kids, too. Come on, we might actually enjoy it."

What sold her in the end were the babysitters. The prospect of being cooped up with the kids at home, when she had so looked forward to getting away, was depressing. So she unpacked her suitcase, putting away all the light, summery things she had planned to wear, and reluctantly switched mental gears for something called a Gateways seminar, in Somerset, New Jersey.

She sighed as she pictured David getting into intense discussions with a bunch of rabbis on topics in which she had zero interest. "It's just three days," she told herself. "Soon it'll be one of those memories that become the stuff of jokes." She wedged in a new bestseller alongside the half dozen magazines she had packed as an antidote to boredom.

At one point during the weekend, however, something about the interaction of the people around her penetrated Lori's aloofness. She was drawn into discussions with people with whom she assumed she had nothing in common. She recalls:

It was shocking to see people meeting each other for the first time, talking from their gut, on an almost intimate level. It jarred me out of my lethargy. For example, one panel discussion focused on how seeking revenge and holding grudges may feel justified but are poison to the mind and soul. A woman in the audience brought this concept into a personal realm. "Can we...can we talk a little bit about the need to forgive not only others but oneself?" she asked haltingly. "How do we forgive ourselves for mistakes that can't be undone?" She flushed as she added, "For me, this is the hardest challenge of all."

Her voice sort of caught, and the room fell silent. Then, one by one, people began offering responses.

Someone said, "That's what Yom Kippur is for. If you know G–d has forgiven you, you can forgive yourself."

"But Yom Kippur comes once a year," someone else protested. "My ulcer can't wait that long!"

When the laughter subsided, the rabbi explained. "Actually, our sages teach there are twelve Yom Kippurs a year. Every Rosh Chodesh, the first day of each new month, is a day to absolve sin, a time of forgiveness."

"Is this penance done through a rabbi?"

"Not at all. In Judaism, repentance and atonement are private. No middlemen are needed. Your relationship with Hashem is exclusive. If you've messed up, it's up to you to work it out with Him."

I wanted to hear more, but the panel discussion finished and the audience dispersed. I inched over to the woman who had asked that anguished question. My heart told me we shared the same "ulcer."

I was right. Before the evening was over, we knew each other's stories. She had been married once before and had a daughter from that marriage from whom she was estranged. She felt a lot of anguish over angry words and hurtful things she had done that had driven a wedge between them. She blamed herself and longed to make peace, but didn't know how.

I listened to her, feeling an odd sensation. We shared the same story, in reverse. My mother had been authoritarian and I was rebellious and headstrong. I broke all the ground rules at home without a shred of remorse. Mom died when I was still in my teens, before we could reconcile. At the time, we were barely speaking to one another. I felt very little grief. I barely mourned for her.

But now, as I heard this woman lament over her daughter's alienation from her, I felt a sweeping sense of regret. My mother, too, must have felt this way! I'd long ago outgrown my resentment of authority and my need to prove myself. Now I wished I had behaved with more compassion for my mother who had tried her best. She had been there for me during trying experiences in my life, even if I didn't appreciate her help at the time.

Suddenly I felt driven to know what Judaism had to say about death and souls, and whether family bonds continue after death. Most of all, I had to know if, according to Jewish belief, anything I might do in this life would have an effect on her soul.

Part of me believed it was too late to reach any closure with my mother. But according to what I was learning at this seminar, the soul lives on after death and travels through time. Certain actions in this world continue to affect it, bringing it peace or distress. I had the sudden intense wish—almost a prayer—that all I was hearing about the soul and the afterlife would turn out to be something more than religious dogma. I so badly wanted it to be *true*.

Gateways opened up a hunger in me that I didn't know I had, the longing to transcend this world and make amends with my mother, to forgive her and to feel forgiven. But I didn't want it to be symbolic, to whisper a few contrite words and consider the case closed. I wanted something concrete and real; something that would have the power on some level to reverse the past.

It was ironic. David was the one who had to convince me to come to the seminar, but I was the one who didn't want it to end. I was beginning to feel that our present lifestyle, for all its rewards and excitement, had its drawbacks. It wasn't just the seminar that brought this home to me. David and I were very successful in our careers, but keeping ourselves on top gave us less and less time for each other. Something in our lives was off balance. At times, I felt like a tightrope walker wobbling on the high wire.

As the weekend drew to a close, the feeling began to grow in me that we needed to continue learning about Judaism and try practicing more of its observances. David was skeptical. His parents are Holocaust survivors and they've always had a kind of love-hate relationship with Judaism. If anything, David wanted less of that kind of religion in his life, not more. I knew I would have to tread carefully.

"If the Torah is true," I ventured to David, after the seminar's closing lecture, "our lives need to take…a different direction."

"I'm not ready to go that far," he said.

"But if a voice from Heaven told you to live a religious life, would you?"

"If a voice from Heaven told me I'm Napoleon, should I go marching off to Waterloo?"

I was quiet. Once he was equating belief in G–d with being delusional, the discussion was basically over.

"There's a difference," I said after a moment. "After everything we heard here, can we just write off the Torah as someone's hallucination?"

"Pretty hard to do that," he conceded. "But that doesn't mean we need to overturn—"

"But what if it's true," I protested, "and G–d said it's forever?"

"Even a document that's 'forever' can be amended or reinterpreted, or even abrogated," my lawyer husband argued.

"Why don't we ask?" I steered him over to one of the Gateways rabbis standing nearby. "Rabbi, how do we know 'forever' in the Torah means forever?"

"Could you fill me in a little on the discussion?" he asked.

He listened to us and answered, "David, you're a lawyer. How long do you think the US Constitution will endure in its present form?"

"I'd say as long as the nation exists," David responded.

"Exactly. Even that man-made document is practically sacrosanct. You have to go through extraordinary efforts to get an amendment ratified. And that's without a mandate from Heaven telling you not to change anything. Apply that mindset to a Divine document that G–d repeatedly promised is as binding and eternal as G–d Himself."

David was silent. I knew what he was thinking. *What in the world did I get myself into here?* This talk about "forever" was unsettling to him. He was flashing me warning looks.

Suddenly a popular ad about diamonds came to my mind: "A

diamond is forever." I had a diamond ring, and David had given me a diamond necklace for our anniversary. It dawned on me that now I wanted a different kind of "diamond." Was the price too high? Our high-powered life left so little time for the things that money can't buy. Where would we have time to fit in Judaism? What would it do to our relationship if one of us believed and the other didn't?

The jury is still out on that one. As a lawyer's wife, though, I've developed a sixth sense about some things....I can sometimes see where the case is going sooner than anyone would think.

❧

David and Lori came back to Gateways a number of weeks later for their first "Gateways Pesach." They stayed for the first five days of Yom Tov. For the first time in their lives, they experienced an authentic Seder. Lori described the encounter as "discovering a parallel universe."

They began to attend classes on Judaism in their neighborhood. With Zachary approaching kindergarten age, the choosing of a school was a turning point for them—forcing them to decide what role they want Judaism to play in their children's lives. Six months later, after a two-week trip to Israel, they were finally able to discuss the issue without sparking an argument.

"Something jelled for David in Israel," Lori said. "It hasn't been an easy decision for either of us: we're in a social and business environment that is not hospitable to Orthodox Judaism, not to mention flak from family members who think we've gone off the deep end. Although we've stopped working on Shabbos and I've begun to use the *mikveh*, we still can't truly define ourselves as completely observant. All I know is that we're on a journey and it's taking us places we never dreamed of going."

Goodbye
to Bizarro

Lisa's Story

People talk a lot about the importance of social skills, about knowing how to fit in, say the right thing, and win acceptance in society. But what if your *society* is crazy?

In my high school years, I felt like the comic book character from the land of Bizarro—the weirdo from a planet where everything is in reverse.

Every decent value was turned on its head in my school. If you got good grades, it's because you wanted to show off; if you were kind, you were a pushover; if you were moral, you were a nerd. Getting laughs by ridiculing other people was a sure route to popularity. Everyone was into drinking parties and a crazy lifestyle. "Lisa, chill out, don't be so inhibited," my classmates would chide. "You gotta be normal. Life ain't a convent."

I could never explain to my worried parents why I had no friends, why the phone never rang for me. My mother pressured me constantly to work my way into the social circle. When I refused, she'd say, "there can't be something wrong with everyone – it must be *you*." She convinced me to go for counseling to discover why I was a loner.

I always longed for a friend, but in high school, today's friend was often tomorrow's enemy, so when you confided in someone, you were taking a real risk. By the end of my high school years, I was in the middle of a full-blown identity crisis. My mother's dictum, "The whole world can't be wrong," was beginning to persuade me that I was nuts. I stopped the counseling because it didn't help; it only made me more confused.

No one ever taught me belief in G–d, so I had no higher moral authority than my parents. My parents had both been raised in non-religious environments but growing up, I remember my family attending a stunning Temple for the High Holidays. Despite their ceremonial aura, the services there were little more than a social event. People yapped right through it and the kids cracked dirty jokes.

In Hebrew school, I had learned to read Hebrew, but never prayed. When my parents divorced after I graduated from high school, I stopped going to synagogue completely. The divorce was a turning point in more than one way for my mother. Shattered and lonely, she turned to religion for comfort. I watched in disbelief as she threw out our old dishes, made the house kosher, started keeping Shabbos. She changed her whole lifestyle. Now, *she* was the square peg.

But instead of welcoming the change, I was bitter that after all the years of her pressuring me to adapt, she finally acknowledged that our world was an unhealthy place. I didn't know how to deal with that sudden reversal. It made me furious. Our relationship grew stormy, and I soon moved out, choosing to live with my father.

It was years before Mom and I reconciled. Only after my father died following a long, lingering illness, was I able to accept her overtures and let our relationship begin to heal.

I had always had a sense of loyalty to Judaism, but was clueless about it. Now, after my father's death, I was struggling with grief and needed to hold onto something. Someone introduced me to Rebbetzin Jungreis' Hineni class, and Tuesday nights soon became the highlight of my week.

Rebbetzin Jungreis had a powerful effect on me. From her class, a series of stepping-stones took me out of darkness. One of these was my introduction to Gateways. I attended a weekend seminar that deeply affected me. At various moments, I looked around me, taking in the wonder of so many people in one place on a quest for truth! There was a unity there, too, and a bonding. At one of the classes over Shabbos, I began to have a glimmer of what my soul had been trying to tell me all those years of being on the outside, never fitting in.

When I walked out of the hotel at the end of the weekend, I was struggling with so many questions. I felt a sudden need to know if any of my relatives had ever lived a Torah life, and why a tradition with so much authentic history behind it had failed to bridge the generations in my own family chain.

From living through a series of bad relationships, I knew what it meant to make or break a commitment. Before I could make a commitment to Torah, I had to know why it had failed my ancestors —or why my ancestors had failed to transmit it.

I began talking to relatives and discovered an amazing thing: my father's father had been religious when he arrived in America from Poland. He came shortly after his bar mitzvah and, fortunately, just a few months before the outbreak of World War II. A picture of him as a young boy showed him wearing a rabbinic-looking black hat (too big for him!), clutching the hand of an older man, a great uncle of mine, who was bareheaded.

This revelation was astounding. My grandfather now lived in Hoboken, New Jersey, and I made a special trip to see him. I had to know the truth. When I brought up the subject, tears came to his eyes. He began reminiscing about his youth in Poland, the way his family lived. He spoke with pride about how he had once known how to learn Torah. He said that for his bar mitzvah he had given a speech on a difficult subject that he had written himself. Back then, he had hopes of one day becoming a rabbi and a scholar.

Brutal anti-Semitism in Poland was seared in his memory. He recalled being pushed into an icy lake by Polish teenagers when he was just five years old. His brother managed to pull him out just in time. Another time, he was dragged off by a Polish neighbor and bruised beyond belief before he finally managed to get away. His mother was urged by friends to take the neighbor to court but was too terrified of reprisals to take any action.

He had difficulty explaining to me why he had turned away from religious practice in America. He was alone in a foreign country, he said, and his experiences in Poland taught him that the last thing he wanted was to stick out as a religious Jew. He had entered the country illegally and never lost his fear of being caught and sent back. Even today—65 years later—he spoke of his illegal entry in a whisper, still fearful of being discovered by authorities.

From the way he spoke, it was obvious that even though his present lifestyle was so different from the way he was raised, his feelings for his childhood and his parents ran very deep. He was curious about my own belated interest in his earlier life. When I told him a little about my exploration of Judaism, his eyes misted.

"Lisa... I should have been the one to inspire you to learn about *Yiddishkeit*. Instead, you're inspiring me. If only I could turn back the clock…who knows? But it's too late for an old man like me."

A lot has happened to me in the past half year. I have my own apartment and I observe Shabbos. The first few times, it was very lonely and depressing. Gradually, I learned that the joy of Shabbos is released when Jews experience Shabbos together, where there is song and friendship and togetherness.

At a Gateways seminar held over Rosh Hashanah, my mother, stepfather, and sister all accompanied me. The experience affected each of us profoundly. My mother and stepfather had been on the brink of divorce. He comes from a religious background, but since adolescence was totally non-observant. At the seminar, something struck a deep chord in him and he and my mother decided to work hard at putting their relationship back on track. When they returned home, they *kashered* the kitchen with the help of a rabbi. They keep Shabbos now, and my stepfather has come full circle. He wears *tzitzis*, he *davens*. We're a family now. It's just incredible.

My own odyssey took me to Israel, where I studied in a seminary for a number of months. I couldn't have done it alone. Rabbi Suchard of Gateways was always there for me, smoothing obstacles, giving advice and encouragement. When I came back to America, one of the first things I did was stop off at a bookstore for some Jewish books. I still mispronounce a lot of words and you can tell I'm a *baalas teshuvah* from a mile away. I don't mind. I'm used to feeling different.

Though I'm a newcomer to religious observance, I feel remarkably comfortable, as though I've come home. It must be in my genes. When I look in the mirror, that angry misfit from Bizarro is no longer staring back at me. That person is gone forever. In her place is the real me, just Lisa, a Jewish daughter with peace and hope in her heart.

Outside, They Were Playing Frisbee

Dan's Story

Some of his buddies had been assigned to Crown Heights during that terrible summer of 1991, when three days of riots terrorized the Jewish community. Hearing them talk about it, Dan was glad he was in a different precinct at the time. He couldn't have stomached the police timidity in the face of thugs assaulting Jews, nor could he comprehend the order not to fire, which enabled the bloodbath to continue.

Dan could feel the terror of the embattled Jewish community. He could picture the hastily assembled Jewish volunteer force trying to provide a net of safety around frightened Jewish families trying to leave town—old people and trembling little children; the desperate wait they had to endure until the authorities came to their senses and brought the violence under control.

And he thought about his parents, Holocaust survivors. Had they lived in Crown Heights, the roving bands of rioters assaulting Jews in broad daylight would have left them paralyzed with terror. So while he was grateful he wasn't there, he also had deep misgivings. Who else but he should have been there to protect these people, his people?

Those thoughts moved Dan to ask for transfer to a different beat, in the heart of religious Brooklyn. Slowly, he came to know the local residents and was surprisingly drawn to certain aspects of Chasidic life. The Chasidim had a naiveté about them mixed with street-smartness. There was a pride in their peculiar dress and lifestyle that he found appealing, even though it made them an easy target for hooligans.

Thinking back to his first experiences in the Brooklyn community, Dan recalled:

Their reaction when they found out I was Jewish always tickled me. Their surprise was mixed with delight, along with a strong handshake as if they were congratulating me. They had all kinds of questions, including nosy, personal ones. They wanted to know not only my name, but my father's name, my grandfather's name, even what town in Europe my parents were from!

I was annoyed at first. But then I realized it was a cultural thing; they didn't know they were prying. Religious Jews always seem to think they might know you from somewhere, or be related to you—or maybe to your grandfather or your great uncle or someone in your family tree. Finding a relative, even a distant one, makes them as excited as kids.

Soon they were inviting me in for *Kiddush* on Shabbos, for a *l'chaim*, for the Shabbos meal, for dessert. The kids couldn't take their eyes off me. Sweet kids. They'd whisper to each other, pointing, staring at me in awe. I guess it was the uniform, the gun belt...

Those same things still make my parents freeze. When I joined the force, we never anticipated that the sight of me in a police uniform would agitate them, reawaken terrifying memories of the Gestapo and the SS. They tried to hide it. They were proud of me and wanted me to know it. But Hitler had gotten to them first. When I visit them, I never, ever walk in with my full uniform on. I always leave the gun and club in the car. I take off my officer's cap, do whatever I can to tone down the effect.

Over the months on the Brooklyn beat, I started to remember bits and pieces of Hebrew and Yiddish, stuff I had learned in the few years I spent in a Jewish school. My parents switched me to public school when I was about ten because I hated being the only kid on the block who had to stay in school till late in the afternoon.

Now, so many years later, watching these little religious kids, five- and six year-olds, reading out of a prayer book, singing Hebrew songs, telling stories from the Torah, I regretted knowing so little. I had no interest in being religious, but I would have at least liked to know how to read Hebrew.

I signed up for a Hebrew crash course in my neighborhood. I was amazed at how reading started coming back to me. It was as though it all had been saved on a file somewhere and I just had to learn how to download it.

I tried to interest Gail, my wife, but reading Hebrew just didn't turn her on. Instead, she started asking questions, tough ones that went to the very heart of the issue. What was the point of learning Hebrew? How do we know the Bible was originally written that way? Even if it were, why not modernize and switch to English? Why insist on studying a book in the original language just because it's 3,000 years old?

The rabbi giving my Hebrew class was a very bright fellow. Instead of tackling everything at once, he gave us some basic information about the Torah and urged us to go to a weekend seminar that would teach a whole lot more about Judaism than just, "Why Hebrew?"

That's how we found Gateways.

There was a warmth at the seminar that I recognized right away. It reminded me of the day a Chasid found out I was Jewish, and that my parents came from a town in Europe called Kalisch. All of a sudden, this total stranger comes over to me and wraps me in a hug! Why? Because his grandfather, no relation of mine, was also from Kalisch! Can you believe it? The bonding among people at the seminar was a lot like that… family discovering family.

Even Gail, who has to know someone really well before she opens up, felt drawn by the camaraderie. Gail comes from a traditional home. Her parents are European like mine, but they came over before the war. An older sister of Gail's married a non-Jew a few years back and it tore her parents apart. It forced Gail to think about loyalty to one's family and religious roots versus the need to follow your own heart.

The classes at the seminar hit us with some real surprises: there are two Torahs! And according to Orthodox belief, the Oral Law is as binding as the Written Law. Who knew?

The speaker, Rabbi Rietti, argued that without the Oral Torah the Bible is incomprehensible. He challenged the audience to prove you could use the written Torah alone as a coherent guide for Jewish living. People immediately cited the Ten Commandments, the dietary laws, the Sabbath and so on.

In each case, the rabbi showed how the Written Torah's instructions are so vague they're almost meaningless. "Must one never kill, even in self-defense? Does the Torah subscribe to pacifism?" he asked. "Where in the Torah does it forbid meat and milk together, or give laws about kosher slaughtering, or how one must honor and observe the Sabbath? Is all this left up to each individual to figure out?"

The Torah was intended to be a highly specific code of laws, the rabbi said. He told us that the basics of the Oral Law, or the Talmud, were given to the Jewish people along with the Written Law and that it provides the answers to all the questions he posed before, in addition to countless others.

Most people in the room with us had never heard of an Oral Law. The rabbi went on to explain how it evolved and was passed down over the ages. With his fascinating sweep of history, he showed us how it was the Oral Law that kept the Jewish people unified through the centuries.

By far, the hardest thing for some people to swallow was that the Bible was dictated by G–d. "Where's the proof?" they wanted to know. "Every religion has its holy book that claims to be the one and only truth."

The rabbis took up the challenge. They pointed out the Torah's claim that the Divine Revelation on Mount Sinai was witnessed by almost three million people—a claim no other religion has ever made. For at least a millennia before Christianity came on the scene, Jews were faithfully telling their children each Passover about their redemption from Egypt, hearing the voice of G–d at Mount Sinai, eating food that fell from the sky…

When millions transmit the same memories to the generations that follow them, that kind of testimony is hard to refute, the speakers pointed out. If the stories were fabricated, skeptics would have torn them apart from the very beginning.

We sat there, taking all this in. There were some spine-tingling moments when it flashed through me that Judaism is a lot more than legends, poetry, and beautiful Bible stories. But it felt so strange. Outside, people were swimming, partying, playing frisbee. They were sitting down to supper, listening to the radio, reading the newspaper. The earth kept spinning on its axis; everything seemed exactly the same. But inside our hotel, something unexpected and a little scary was happening.

Gail and I were hard-hit with new ideas coming faster than we could digest them. We were high on inspiration, but had no idea what to do with the insights we had gained. Gail particularly disliked the implications of the Torah being "absolute truth." She had walked into the seminar expecting an interesting social and intellectual experience and hadn't bargained on having her world turned upside down. Where would all this take us?

ﾏ

Gateways kept in touch with Dan and Gail in the weeks and months following the seminar. Over the next few months, follow-up study sessions were set up at the couple's request in Chumash, Jewish law, and hashkafah. It was a time of growth, experimentation, and change. For Pesach, after much discussion and soul-searching, Dan and Gail kashered their home. A year and many milestones later, they returned to Gateways, bringing with them fifteen relatives and watching with excitement as "family discovered family."

Rocky Mountain High

Jill's Story

As a young girl, I used to watch my father write out checks to people who came to the door collecting for charity. Sometimes he would lend money to people too, remarking to me over his shoulder that Jews are kind and ethical people, that we must care about others.

That was the sum total of my Jewish education. But Dad's compassion made a lasting impression on me: he embodied what I assumed to be the essence of Judaism. I tried to follow his example.

In college, I was teased for being the "Queen of Self-Improvement." I was into every self-improvement fad around. *The Seven Habits of Highly Effective People* was only one of my many "Bibles."

I never looked inside the real Bible, though, until much later in life. I was married then, and belonged to a Reform temple led by a woman rabbi, where the women read from the Torah on Shabbat. I had learned to read Hebrew for my Confirmation so it was not that hard for me to learn how to chant the Torah portion, something I found deeply fulfilling.

Once, at a lecture on Jewish Women and Judaism given by Dr. Lisa Aiken, I mentioned during the discussion period that although I was not observant, I read aloud from the Torah on Shabbat, and this made me feel close to G–d. Dr. Aiken's response stunned me. She said, "Your feeling of being connected to G–d is only the tiniest glimmer of what a real relationship with Him would feel like. The closeness to G–d that would come from *observing* the Torah—not just reading from it —would be infinitely deeper. You cannot imagine what it is like until you do it."

She continued talking about the Torah as a Divine set of instructions meant to guide every Jew in day-to-day life. We could not fathom G–d's reasons for the commandments, she said, but since they came from G–d Himself, they are perfect and eternal.

I came home in tears. I felt so deflated and hurt. But along with a profound sense of disappointment was also the thrill of having stumbled across something mysterious that I longed to know more about: G–d wanted something from me as a Jewish woman, a Jewish mother and wife—something more than just being a good person. The thought was both exhilarating and terrifying.

I never returned to our temple. Dr. Aiken had opened my eyes to the hollowness of the Judaism I had known until now. It suddenly struck me as bizarre that the subject of G–d was consistently avoided in our temple. The congregation outwardly venerated the Torah, but ignored its contents. Why then did they go through the whole fanfare of taking the Torah out of the Ark and reading aloud from it? If it's nothing but fables and archaic laws, what's the point?

Things that my husband and I had turned a blind eye to suddenly seemed intolerable. For example, a woman who gave Hebrew classes at the temple to young children openly practiced a deviant lifestyle and actually brought up the subject in her classes. No one else seemed to think there was anything wrong with this, but we were shocked. At first, I tried to suppress my disgust for the sake of tolerance. But a parent's primal instinct is to protect her child: By violating my child's innocence, the temple had shattered my trust.

Leaving our temple was not difficult, but it put us at a crossroads. Where to go from here?

The first thing we did was to take our son out of the Hebrew school he was in. Since there was no other Jewish school, we decided to home-school him. An outreach program in our town put me in touch with a young man from Israel who was religiously and secularly educated, and he agreed to tutor my son in a number of subjects. This young man, in turn, introduced my husband and me to the nearby religious community in Denver.

It's strange how many influences converged at this point to steer us on our spiritual journey. We spent a Shabbos in Denver as guests of a religious family and met their rabbi, Rabbi Myer, as well as other members of the *shul*.

With the same instant flash of intuition I had experienced with Dr. Aiken, I knew that we belonged in Denver with these warm and committed people. Many people extended themselves to us in the following months, hosting our family of six Shabbos after Shabbos, and for many of the holidays. The sense of caring in that close-knit community was a powerful draw.

The greatest trial my husband and I faced at this point was our vastly different levels of commitment. Mark did not share my eagerness to turn over our lives and become religious. He felt no emotional tug and urged me to take things much more slowly. A religious synagogue was such a far cry from what we had been used to. At first, he flatly refused to accompany me there.

We had some heated arguments. At one point, when I was ready to embrace Shabbos observance, I said, "Mark, could we try not to use electricity this Shabbos?"

"I'm not ready for that," was his stony reply.

But I took out adhesive tape anyway and I taped up some light switches. "Look," I said, "if you can't manage and you want to turn the light on or off, go ahead and do it. But at least let's try it."

This was typical of the way things went, and looking back, I can't say I'm proud of it. I was impulsive and impatient, eager to do things in a sweeping, all-consuming way. It wasn't fair to Mark. But I had 38 years of missing out on what Judaism has to offer and felt I couldn't waste any more time.

Mark Recalls

For a while, Jill and I were on very different pages and things were definitely rough. The turning point for me came at a Gateways seminar we attended in the Colorado Rockies about two years ago. It made a strong impact on our entire family, but for me, particularly, it was a pivotal experience.

The classes and seminars offered a rational approach to believing in G–d and in the Torah that was completely new to me. It was refreshing to meet such intelligent rabbis who used humor and sensitivity to open up our horizons. It was their gentle way of allowing us to form our own conclusions rather than being told what we should believe. That approach drew me into the Torah's orbit.

Even the children's program opened a window to religious values. We were deeply impressed by the kindness showered on our kids. The Gateways staff taught our children beautiful Shabbos songs that they continue to sing to this day. Without a television, video, MP3 or a single electronic toy, they kept the children engrossed in activities all Shabbos long.

About a year after the Rocky Mountain Gateways seminar, Jill and I began to debate whether to pull up stakes from our upscale Glendale Village neighborhood and move to Denver. We were torn between conflicting priorities. The house in Glendale Village was our dream house, a real step-up house. I loved it. Jill loved it. But we needed a good Jewish school for our children, and we needed a Jewish community for ourselves. It was an agonizing decision. In the end, we put our home up for sale and rented an apartment in Denver.

Hashem gave us plenty of time to reconsider—and we almost did. Real estate had plunged and we couldn't unload the house for anything close to what it was worth. The house was on the market for eight months. We finally decided to sell it at a loss so we could buy a new home in Denver.

For people like us who grew up without the security of faith, making a spiritual move that came at such a steep price was very difficult. But one thing I have learned: the rewards, when they come, are so rich that you wonder why you ever hesitated.

One day, I asked my six year-old if he was scared by the thunder and lightning the night before. "I wasn't afraid because Hashem is watching over us," he answered simply.

Tears came to my eyes. My little boy had learned a beautiful language that was still a struggle for his parents. My child already knew what it took us half a lifetime to find out. For one long moment, he was the parent and I, the child. I was so grateful that he had the opportunity to grow up this way. I knew then that Jill and I would do whatever it would take to make our home a bulwark for his faith—and ours.

From
Kiev to
Jerusalem

Hannah's Story

My grandmother saw family, friends, and neighbors dragged away by Nazi soldiers and Ukrainian thugs in her home city of Kiev. Hour after hour, sounds of machine gun fire coming from the outskirts of town filled her ears, as she lay hidden.

Pregnant at the time, she was separated during the turmoil from her husband and four children. At one point, she was wounded by gunfire and left for dead.

Later, she found out that the Jewish victims had been forced to the edge of a gorge called Babi Yar, where they were mowed down into the ravine. Thousands of men, women, and children were murdered this way. Her husband and children died in the bloodbath.

But she survived.

Babi Yar was a name that filled me with terror from the time I was very little. I knew it was about something unfathomably evil. I knew that it haunted my mother, that the pain of Babi Yar was always lurking somewhere under the surface. She never spoke to me about it. I had to wait till I was an adult to find out what it was.

Grandmother remarried after the war and gave birth to my mother while still living in Kiev. Growing up in the shadow of the Holocaust, my mom remembers a childhood clouded by fear. For a Jew living in Kiev under the Soviet regime, life was oppressive. Jew-baiting and harassment were the norm.

"There were so few of us. I had only one Jewish friend and we stuck together," she recalled. It was the two of them against hostile classmates. Life at school became so miserable that her parents had to send her away. She traveled a long distance to a school far away from home, where her Jewish identity was unknown.

When my parents immigrated to America as a young couple, they longed to blend into the American landscape. They hoped that their two children, my brother and I, would escape the bitter persecution both of them had suffered.

We never kept any Jewish holidays or customs. Except for giving charity to Israel, my parents distanced themselves from other Jews. I absorbed the message from earliest childhood that the road to prosperity was to become fully American, to play down my Russian background and my Jewish roots.

I went through high school and college without questioning this message. The first time I challenged it was at an encounter with the Gateways Organization at a weekend seminar just over a year ago.

That seminar opened up the world of Judaism to me. Mrs. Greenblatt's class on Jewish womanhood touched something deep inside. I felt she was reading the secrets of my heart.

Another class, taught by Rabbi Kohl, made the concept of prayer very real and personal. He said that, in essence, "you pray what you are and you are what you pray." Your deepest prayer is a signpost to your truest self. Through prayer to the One Above, you come to know who you really are.

I had never prayed before that weekend. I knew nothing about G–d. The idea that He wanted my "conversation," or that my speaking to Him could accomplish anything concrete, was novel to me.

Another awakening: I discovered that keeping kosher had a science to it. It was more than a bunch of ancient taboos. I had always known about religious Jews keeping kosher because when my mom reminisced about life under Communism, she often commented that she never tasted meat as a child because the Soviets made it impossible for Jews to get kosher meat.

How ironic, she said, that once they were in America, they could finally eat kosher, she and my father never bothered to. They no longer practiced Judaism. "How strange life is," she would sigh. "My mother would have been so grateful for kosher food."

I left that seminar intrigued and stimulated, and wanting to learn more. The Gateways staff set me up with a phone partner to learn Hebrew and invited me to follow- up seminars and classes. Six months later, I found myself with a group of Russian-American Jewish college students like myself at another weekend retreat. We felt an immediate cultural affinity to one another. There was also an emotional bond that came from similarities in our parents' way of raising us, and their goals of seeing their children succeed.

Part of that ambition included keeping our Jewishness under lock and key so it wouldn't hinder us socially. By getting deeper into Judaism, we were all breaking an unspoken taboo. We knew our parents didn't approve, yet it felt tremendously liberating.

When I first decided to keep kosher, I had been going to classes and Shabbatons for several months at RAJE, a Gateways branch for Russian American Jews in Brighton Beach. For me, keeping kosher was not only about observing the Torah. It was my way of hitting back at the people who had made the lives of my parents and grandparents in Russia so miserable.

At the time I began to eat kosher, I was studying social work. My college pals were an important part of my life and eating out together was part of our lifestyle. Mother cautioned me not to stand out as a Jew by refusing to join my friends at restaurants and pizza parlors. "You will lose every friend you have," she warned me.

I grew used to her radiating disapproval over my becoming too Jewish, and to her dire warnings that I would suffer for it in the end. Sometimes I ignored her; sometimes I answered her sharply. One day, something unexpected happened that moved me deeply. Mom came home from the store with new pots and pans for me. "We'll cook only kosher in them," she promised me with a wan smile. I hugged her. Courage had won out over fear.

I can't say the transition to kosher was easy, but at the same time, I was forging friendships with other students at RAJE. Together, we were emerging into a sense of Jewish identity and feeling proud of it.

I began to experiment with keeping Shabbos, a little bit at a time. One day, I realized that I reached the point of no return. The luxury of "experimenting" was no longer mine. Something had shifted inside me. I no longer had the freedom to pick up my pocketbook or snap on the light on Shabbos.

This came as a shock to me and I fought it. On Shabbos, I moved toward the light switch to prove I could still exercise a choice, but the anxiety I felt made me stop immediately. At first, I was distraught at the realization that I had lost my freedom. I wanted to turn back the clock. But it was too late. Shabbos was Shabbos whether I liked it or not. I needed to "do Shabbos" the right way in order to feel at peace with myself.

This past summer, I went with RAJE on their Fellowships program to Israel and Europe. The two-week trip combined touring with classes and social events. We all fell in love with Israel. I would ride the bus to the Western Wall at night, soaking in the beauty of the Old City ... the lights in the valleys and hills twinkling in the darkness, merging with the stars.

Looking upwards, I felt my heart open. Everything I was learning about G–d and the Torah and the Jewish people were concentrated here. I felt the enormous weight of Jewish history and an extraordinary joy in being a Jewish woman with a Jewish destiny.

At Yad Vashem, I stood in shock before the searing footage of Jews being shot in cold blood in the killing fields of the Ukraine. A tall, rabbinic looking Jew was captured on film removing his coat before an open grave, as Germans kept their guns trained on him.

My heart stopped. I turned to stone. I had come face to face with my mother's nightmare.

When I came home, I was no longer the same person. Feelings and decisions about what I wanted to do with my life had become clear to me. I decided to tackle Hebrew in earnest. I knew it would be an uphill struggle. I was working on my doctorate and had to meet deadlines. But I also knew it was time for me to learn how to read from a *siddur*. The next time I visit the Kotel, I decided, I will know how to pray as a Jew should.

There was something else I wanted to do. I wanted to sign up for one of the tours to Europe I'd seen advertised. I was finally ready to go to my mother's homeland. I knew she wouldn't accompany me, so I would confront her ghosts myself.

Trembling and terrified, I would stand at Babi Yar. I would say a prayer for the slain Jews whose bones were ground to dust by the Nazis determined to leave no trace of the slaughter.

Some of those victims were my family. I might never have known how they lived or died. I might never have realized my responsibility to keep their memory, their faith, and their way of life alive.

I might have lived out my parents' vision of an all-American daughter who had no links to her parents' traumatic past. Maybe that would have worked for all of us, for a while. But in the end, a person needs more than material success; she needs to know where her story began. Only then can she find the thread connecting herself from the past to the present. Only then will that present have meaning and light the way to the future.

My Daughter,
My Teacher

Rob's Story

It all began the day Mindy, our fifth grade daughter, came home on the warpath. Her class at Edgewood Elementary School had begun practicing that day for a school choir. It was to be part of a school-wide performance coinciding with the December holiday season.

"I don't want to be in the choir," my daughter said defiantly. "They can't make me."

"Why not?" I asked. "You like to sing."

"They're Christmas songs!"

I turned to my wife, baffled. We're Jewish and proud of it but Christmas carols are a part of American culture. True, the department stores overdid it, playing the music ad nauseam, but there are times when even I caught myself humming some of those tunes.

"Hmm. Christmas carols. Is that such a big deal?" I asked.

"Yes, it is! I'm not going to sing them!"

My wife, Lily, said, "Rob, she has a point. Look at this song sheet. These are religious songs—almost like church hymns."

I scanned the song sheet. She was right. I looked over at Mindy, whose small face was set in hard lines. Generally sweet-tempered, she looked angry and hurt. Something more must have happened at school to trigger this uncharacteristic belligerence.

"Honey, did you refuse to sing the songs in school?" I asked her.

She nodded as tears sprang into her eyes.

"So what happened?"

"My teacher got angry. She said everyone has to participate. But Daddy, if I'm Jewish, why do I have to sing Christian songs?"

The Jewish pride I saw in her eyes moved me and made me feel ashamed. I knew I couldn't take the credit for it. Lily and I practiced Judaism in the casual way we had seen it practiced in our own homes. Bits and pieces, here and there. No logic or consistency to it. Kosher in the home, McDonald's outside. Lily lit Shabbat candles Friday night, but that was it. That's the Judaism I myself grew up with. Until I reached adulthood, I never heard of the concept of not working on Shabbos and holidays.

After my bar-mitzvah, I dropped Jewish observance completely. By the time I was in college, even the High Holidays meant nothing to me. At least six of my cousins married non-Jews and no one saw anything wrong with it. Lily's Jewish background was very similar to mine. But because she happens to be more of a spiritual person, she's always been drawn to learning about Judaism.

My daughter, Mindy, takes after her. The oldest of our three children, she's aflame about anything Jewish. Since the age of seven, she attended Sunday school classes sponsored by our temple. She'll come home brimming with excitement about Jewish holidays and rituals. She even asked to go to a Jewish day school but Lily and I decided against it. The public schools in our district have high academic standards. We saw no reason to pay seven or eight thousand dollars in yearly tuition for a private school.

"If I went to a Jewish school, I wouldn't have this problem," Mindy said bleakly. Her sadness made me flinch. What could I say? She was right. A girl like this belonged in a Jewish school.

"How about if I go down to the school and have a talk with the principal?" I suggested. My daughter wiped her eyes and nodded.

I was pretty confident of being able to reach an understanding with Dr. Brenner, the principal of Edgewood Elementary. We had once served on a town committee together and he struck me as a reasonable fellow. I intended to ask him to alter the religious agenda of the program, and if that wasn't possible, to exempt my daughter and other Jewish students who found it offensive.

I was shocked to find out that beneath the veneer of congeniality, the man was intolerant and overbearing. He not only refused to consider changing the choir's religious overtones, he insinuated that my daughter would become "socially ostracized" if she didn't participate.

"Is that a warning to expect religious harassment?" I asked.

"Don't play the "religious harassment" card with me, Mr. Wasserman," he snapped back. "That won't get you far. Instead of dictating to us how we should run our school, you might want to consider moving your daughter to an environment where she'd be with her own kind."

He was clearly a religious bigot. I came home seething. By the next morning, I'd hired a civil rights lawyer to sue the school for violating my constitutional rights. My lawyer believed we had an excellent case. He gave me the task of collecting signatures for a petition against Edgewood Elementary for foisting religious indoctrination on its students. As the student body of the school was at least 25 percent Jewish, I thought I'd have no problem. I was dead wrong. The Jewish parents were afraid to get involved. "Don't rock the boat," I was advised. "You're fighting the wrong fight."

But I was in too deep to back down. After seeing what went on at Edgewood Elementary, I felt it was critical to focus public attention on the administration's infringement of the rights of its Jewish students. These kids needed the protection that a court decision would afford.

So I ignored the advice of people who, instead of encouraging me, warned me that I was stirring up anti-Semitism in our community. Lily, too, got phone-calls from "friends" who referred to me as "hotheaded" and "reckless." Sad to say, the harshest criticism we faced in our efforts to protect Jewish kids was from Jews!

Then, with the concert just three days away—and a court date looming just two weeks after that—I received the biggest surprise of all: a phone call from the mayor of the town. He wanted to meet with me to see if we could work out a compromise, to avoid a trial that he said would "give the community a black eye."

I said the time for compromise was over; I wasn't going to be sucked into quibbling over this or that song. I told the mayor that I would withdraw the lawsuit on one condition only: that he cancel the fifth grade concert in its entirety. He took an injured tone and accused me of wanting to "retaliate" against an entire class of children over my own "petty intolerance."

On the day of the performance, I sat with my wife and daughter in the audience holding a video recorder, intending to video the performance for the benefit of the judge during our upcoming day in court. A minute passed, then two. The announcer appeared on stage. He stammered an apology to the audience for an unexpected change in the program, explaining that "due to time constraints, the fifth grade choir was being rescheduled and would perform at a later date."

As we made our way out of the theater, a number of Jewish parents in the audience quietly came over to me, whispering "Congratulations, Rob!" and "Mazel tov!" as they pumped my hand.

Ironically, among them were some who had bitterly opposed me. "Thanks—you're a little late," I wanted to tell them.

We had clearly won the battle but after the dust settled, we had to face the practical outcome of this victory. Our girls needed a new school. Mindy wanted to attend Maimonides Academy, a religious day school on the outskirts of town that drew its students predominantly from the small but growing Orthodox community. The principal, Rabbi

Safir, interviewed both her and my younger daughter, Sara, who was in third grade and told me, "We'd love to have them, but they need to catch up on some basics first. They'll be lost in class."

Lily and I agreed. We weren't at all sure the school was suitable for other reasons. How could we transition our girls so abruptly into a religious environment that was so radically different from what they were used to? Lacking a good alternative in town, we considered home-schooling the girls.

But we hadn't bargained on their determination. Mindy insisted on trying out the Academy, and her sister followed her lead. We finally relented because that seemed the only way to prove to them that the school would not meet their needs.

Well, they proved us wrong. In three months, they had leap-frogged ahead in their studies and were holding their own pretty well academically, and socially, too. It was amazing how easily they made friends here!

But this transition was not without its speed bumps. Mindy was enraptured by the Orthodox lifestyle. She wanted her parents to embrace it as well. I'd be getting ready to drive to temple Saturday morning as she gazed outside in fascination as our new neighbors, the Leiders, passed our house on their trek to the Orthodox synagogue. Rain or shine, no matter what the weather, they strolled and skipped along. Children dressed up as if going to a wedding. Mother and father clasping the little ones' hands, laughing and talking.

Mindy begged Lily and me to try out the Orthodox synagogue with her. The idea of walking almost a mile to get anywhere, let alone an Orthodox synagogue, was not in the least inviting but I finally agreed. Waking up Shabbat morning to frigid rainy weather, though, I lost my nerve. Mindy still wanted to go, but when she reminded me that we couldn't use an umbrella, I put my foot down. "What's wrong with an umbrella?" I demanded, bracing myself for more Orthodox dogma. She didn't know.

This was typical of our encounter with Orthodox Judaism and it naturally caused some tension. Whatever changes Lily and I made seemed to fall short of Mindy's expectations. It wasn't enough that now we ate only kosher at home, and agreed not to drive or use the phone or turn on lights on Shabbos. It wasn't enough that the TV and radio were silent all day.

I'd come home a few minutes before sundown Friday afternoon to find Mindy red-eyed, as if she'd been crying. "What's wrong?" I'd ask her, alarmed.

"I was worried you wouldn't get home on time. Why can't you come home earlier for Shabbos? You're not even ready!" she'd blurt out, tears rolling down her face.

Ironically, it was the very same neighbors who so intrigued my daughter who came to the rescue! After we became friendly with them, they introduced us to the Gateways Organization, a Jewish outreach group that runs seminars and classes for people who want to learn more about Judaism. Gateways literally opened a new chapter in our lives.

At our first seminar, we were placed for the Friday night meal at the same table as one of the staff members and his family. I watched the father make *kiddush*, then bless his children afterward, hugging and kissing each one. Looking around, I saw similar scenes unfolding at other tables.

Tears stung my eyes as memories from so long ago awakened. A sudden vision of my grandfather lovingly performing this same ritual with my brother and me swept away the present. There were no snapshots of those scenes in the family album and I'd long ago forgotten them.

We're little kids, my brother and I, about 8 and 6. Grandpa is standing by the table singing Shalom Aleichem, *with me on his right and my brother on his left. He cradles our shoulders with his strong arms, and we nestle against him, singing along at the top of our lungs. Grandma joins in, laughing, eyes misting with tears. Grandpa makes kiddush and hands us small silver cups of wine to drink. He blesses us... We don't understand the words but we feel the love. In the morning, he takes us to shul with him and shows us off to his friends.*

Shabbos in my grandparents' home was a tangible, loving presence. You walked into the house and felt it in the air; you could smell and taste it. You missed it when it slipped away at night.

When my grandparents passed away, it was if Shabbos itself vanished. I never experienced it again with that incredible sweetness and forgot it even existed. Until now. Savoring the long-lost memories, I finally had a glimmer of what my daughter craved.

Lily and I reacted very strongly to the first seminar. We were astounded at how deep Judaism is, how we had grown up with not more than a tiny skewed glimpse of what it's all about. Learning about the deeper wisdom in the Alef-Bet was mind-boggling. With so much richness embedded in a single letter, the Torah itself had to be absolutely surreal. The argument that the Torah with all its myriad laws and guidelines applies to modern times, didn't go down easily. But the speakers defended this position with logic, not emotion. It was very compelling.

We attended classes back to back and would meet in the tea room to share impressions. We met people like ourselves who were searching for clarity, and friendships blossomed on the spot.

We knew that we'd reached a turning point when, on the way home from the seminar, I found some sandwiches from McDonald's in the car, leftovers from the day before that were still quite edible. I picked up one and just kind of looked at it. "You know something?" I turned to Lily. "I think it would be most appropriate to take this thing and throw it out the window."

"Throw them all out," she said. "Just find a trash can first."

⁊⸰

Rob gave this interview eleven years after he and Lily attended the first of many Gateways seminars and retreats. Since then, they and their children embarked on what he calls "an amazing journey," becoming fully mitzvah observant as well as loyal members of the Torah community.

Rob attributes their steady growth in Yiddishkeit *in large measure to Mindy's "leading the way for the family." He also credits the immense influence of the many classes and programs hosted by Gateways, and the close bonds that developed between himself and Lily and the Gateways staff.*

"Rabbi Suchard, Rabbi Rietti, Rabbi Becher, Rabbi Jordan… they're like extended family to us," he says.

Rob has written his own fascinating page in the annals of Torah learning and outreach. In addition to his own k'vius in learning, he recently inaugurated a Thursday night learning program at his son's yeshiva, where fathers and sons come to learn Mishnayos. *Rob awards the boys valuable prizes for steady attendance and for making* siyumim. *He has also perfected technology to provide, free of charge, live interactive video conferencing for* shiurim *in Israel that are broadcast to locations in the United States and Europe.*

Worlds Apart

Cindy's Story

When I remarried fourteen years ago, I made a major concession to my husband, Jack, never dreaming it would cause me to lose one of my children: I agreed to keep a kosher home. I submitted to this even though I belonged to a Reform temple where keeping kosher, while not actually disqualifying you for membership, made you the butt of patronizing jokes.

Keeping kosher is easy, my Conservative husband promised me. But it was not easy for me in the least. The hardest part was trying to convince my fifteen-year-old daughter, Julie, to abide by the deal. She wanted no part of it, and took every opportunity to flaunt her disdain.

Jack would come across the wrappers from bacon or non-kosher franks she left around and there would be fireworks. Julie, who was going through a lot of turmoil at that time, showed no remorse. She had no intention of having religion rammed down her throat, she said, and threatened to leave home and go live with her father, my ex-husband.

When she made good on her threat, I was devastated. Jack advised me not to run after her. He felt certain that Julie would come back once she saw we were united on the ground rules in the house. Unfortunately, he was wrong. Julie stayed away. Although we called each other and once in a while met for lunch, she refused to step foot in my house for five years.

To my great sadness and regret, I missed out on those adolescent years when a girl needs a mother—and a mother takes such pride in a maturing daughter. The choice I had to make between my daughter and my marriage left an open wound for many years.

I thought it was a terrible price to pay for keeping kosher, something which had no intrinsic value to me. I was furious at the Jewish laws, and I was furious at my husband for going about the whole issue of religion in such an irrational, dogmatic way. He himself knew very little about Judaism, beyond the ritual aspects, so he could never explain, to me or to Julie, what was so important about keeping kosher.

I already had one broken marriage behind me, partly because I had been too rigid and unable to compromise. I couldn't let that happen to me again. So I kept my part of the deal faithfully, and Jack, in turn, made no further religious demands. He'd go off to services Saturday morning, saying, "Cindy, I'm going now…" There was an unspoken question in the air: "Why don't you come along?" But I'd say breezily, "I'm on my way out, too. I'm getting my hair done this morning."

Gradually, Jack moved even more to the right and joined a small synagogue led by an Orthodox rabbi. They'd be holding some sort of class or evening affair and he'd encourage me to come with him, but I'd always find an excuse to decline. The thought of actually going into an Orthodox synagogue killed any desire I might have had to learn about Judaism.

I'd heard all about it from friends who had been there: the separation of husbands from wives, the Hebrew services, women in long skirts. This was not a user-friendly religion.

Meanwhile, I started noticing something strange about my youngest son, Danny, who was in second grade in a Jewish day school. He had always been an easy child, but he started becoming difficult in the middle of the year. First he balked at going out to eat with us. He decided he didn't want to eat hamburgers—his favorite food—in restaurants anymore, because Jews are not allowed to eat *treife*. At times he agreed to eat pizza. And if there was no pizza, he would eat nothing. At one point, he announced that he wouldn't go "trick or treating" on Halloween because it wasn't a Jewish holiday and "Jews don't celebrate non-Jewish holidays."

I was very upset with the school for creating conflict in my son about our lifestyle. A friend advised me to say nothing to the school but simply bide my time until Halloween. "As soon as he sees the candy and treats the other kids have," she counseled, "he'll forget the teachers' nonsense."

So I did just that. I bought an expensive Nintendo costume and hung it in Danny's closet. I bought loads of candy and chocolate, knowing how kids love to compare the goodies they're going to get and give out. I even decorated the house with a jack-o-lantern and a few goblins.

Well, the whole thing fell flat. My son not only wasn't impressed or tempted, he was saddened by all the fanfare. He didn't even look at the costume and he didn't seem to care that he was missing out on all the loot.

I couldn't believe how much power Danny's teachers had over him. I knew I had to watch this thing very carefully because who knew how far it could go? What if this was some kind of cult? Switching Danny against his will to another school might have been an option if I had my husband's cooperation. But Jack welcomed Danny's interest in Judaism and saw nothing extreme about it.

Besides, the public school in our area was academically inferior so I couldn't consider transferring my son there. Jewish parents in the neighborhood—even those who were totally secular—chose the day school for their kids because of its higher standards, even though they didn't care for its religious orientation.

By the time Danny was in third grade, he refused to watch television or listen to music on Shabbos. He had stopped going to synagogue with my husband because the synagogue was not in walking distance. Eventually, Jack too, stopped driving on Shabbos and began talking about moving to a different neighborhood where we'd be closer to the synagogue.

I felt the fabric of our family and social life unraveling. I was alternating between outrage, helplessness, and a desire to understand my child's inner world—a world that operated by rules I couldn't fathom.

To my husband's immense credit, he never gave me the sense that he was "teaming up" with Danny against me, although it was clear they shared something I was not a part of. Instead, Jack continued encouraging me to attend some of the classes the synagogue held so I could meet the people. "They're just a nice bunch of people. You'll like them. Trust me," he'd say.

To make him happy, I finally agreed to try a class on Jewish history. Despite my apprehensions, I was surprised to find the women in the group congenial. The second time I went, there was a discussion in progress about setting up a weekly home-study group in a centrally located place. On an impulse, I offered our home as the meeting place. Jack was convinced I was joking when I told him.

There was no great mystery behind this turn-around. I had begun to realize that there were two options before me: I could be stubborn and stupid and lose my son the way I had lost my daughter. Or I could put myself in Danny's place and try to feel what it must be like for him to feel connected and secure in his Jewish identity—but thwarted by a mother who refused to comprehend.

The class got off the ground right away. A woman from an outreach group called Gesher taught about Jewish holidays and other subjects, all completely new to me. That class was my stepping stone to another outreach organization, Gateways.

I went to my first Gateways seminar with a certain amount of trepidation. When I saw the religious-looking staff—women in long skirts and the men in black and white—alarms started ringing in my head. "This must be a money-making organization," I thought, wondering when we would be hit with the fundraising pitch, and when they would start their proselytizing.

But none of that happened. What we found instead were

intelligent and thoughtful people who were well acquainted with our world. They were so open, you could ask them anything, including why religious people lent themselves to such negative stereotypes.

I remember that one participant did just that. He commented that Orthodox Jews seem to feel they have a monopoly on the truth and he pointed out the anomaly there. "If most of the world rejects your views," he said bluntly, "wouldn't the odds indicate that you are wrong? After all, the whole world can't be wrong. No offense intended," he added after a moment.

The rabbi seemed to be suppressing a smile. "On the contrary, the whole world can indeed be wrong. The whole world once believed in paganism. In Nazi Germany, the "whole world" proclaimed that Jews were evil and had to be killed. To someone living in Russia at the height of the Communist era, "the whole world" was embracing Communism. History has shown that the truth at times has been in the sole possession of a small minority.

"So, no—we Jews are not fazed by the fact that the world does not agree with us," he said. "That doesn't surprise or confuse us in the slightest."

There was humor, laughter, eye-opening revelations about Judaism and most of all, an ambience that melted the barriers between people and made you feel deep-down good about being Jewish. Jack, Danny and I hadn't felt so together about something in a very long time. I went to classes on *kashrus* and Shabbos and for the first time began to see some coherence and logic in the laws. I found myself thinking, "If someone had explained all this to me a long time ago, I wouldn't have fought it so hard."

It wasn't that I suddenly wanted to be a religious Jew, but I could now understand that living that way was not cultish or stupid or primitive. It was a matter of believing that G–d communicated these laws to the Jewish people and wanted them to be kept for eternity. To be honest, never in my life had I heard the concept that G–d actually handed down these laws Himself. Even in the heat of my arguments with Jack about the *kashrus* issue, he never brought up the most obvious argument: he never said, "Because G–d wants it this way."

I began to understand why Danny loved what he learned in the day school. And I began to feel proud that—as one of the rabbis put it—"he has a *neshamah* that is asking for holiness."

So much has changed in a few short years that it's incredible. To begin with, we now live in Yardley, Pennsylvania, where we joined a wonderful community of over 35 families, all newcomers to Orthodox Judaism and members of the same *shul*, whose rabbi, Rabbi Yitzchok Feldheim, is also a Gateways lecturer.

All of us here have gone through our own personal journey to reach this point, and many of us have had to leave family members behind, both literally and symbolically. The rifts that are created when some family members cannot forgive you for growing in Jewish faith and observance may heal over time, but it is terribly sad and painful while you remain estranged.

Jack, Danny and I have been to a number of Gateways seminars, in addition to attending follow-up classes and home-study programs over the course of several years. We owe Rabbi Suchard and the staff so much. We feel like family there. For a long time I harbored a secret hope that I could somehow persuade Julie to come to a seminar. I tried to talk to her a few times, but she wouldn't hear of it. "I don't consider myself Jewish," she said. "We are worlds apart. I don't believe in organized religion, period."

Friday night when I light candles I keep in mind that this is the most propitious moment to ask Hashem for what you need. I've begged Him to help Julie return to Judaism. Not for selfish reasons—wanting her to live like me or be like me—but because I know it would bring her peace of mind, something she has searched the world for and has yet to find.

Just last week, Julie finally let me talk her into coming to a seminar with us. We made plans for one in November. The very fact that she agreed to come is a small miracle. I have faith that Hashem will grant us an even bigger one and help Julie become part of our family again.

Cross-Generation Redemption

Yael's Story

At the age of 78, my mother had survived two cardiac arrests, triple-bypass surgery, and a serious fall which put her into a body cast for six months. But it was the next crisis—kidney failure and congestive heart failure combined—that was the most severe. The outcome of that ordeal shattered a decision she had made almost 60 years earlier in the ashes of the Holocaust.

Mother survived the war by posing as a relative of a Christian family who hid her Jewish identity from the neighbors. At the war's end, she and her twelve-year-old brother, Avrohom, who had been in hiding elsewhere, were reunited with their mother who had survived the death camps.

The three made their way to Israel with thousands of other refugees as soon as the ports of Palestine were opened. They lived through the Israeli War of Independence and the chaotic years that followed, deeply grateful to be in a land where Jews were free.

The tragic thing was that hiding out as a Christian child for three years had wiped away my mother's Jewish identity. Even after the war was over, she did not resume a religious lifestyle as her brother did. Her grandfather had been a rabbi in Vienna and her family was one of the most respected in the religious community. But she wanted a complete break with her terrifying past.

That decision caused tremendous friction between her and my grandmother, who kept a strictly religious home as she had in Vienna before the war. Things got worse between them when my mother married a man who shared her need to break away from a religious way of life.

My father, who had grown up in a religious home in Budapest, Hungary, had gone through his own ordeal during the war. He was sent to be gassed, but moments before his group was shoved into the gas chamber, he darted away. SS guards shot at him and chased him with dogs. Bleeding and wounded, he managed to escape. It meant going through barbed wire and staying hidden for days with nothing to eat. To this day, I don't know how he did it. He never went into the details of that terrifying escape. A farmer found him, helped him recover from his wounds, and hid him from the SS. After the war, he immigrated to Israel.

Because of my grandmother's deep disappointment in my parents' secular lifestyle, they kept their distance from her. I was strangely drawn to my grandmother and loved receiving letters and gifts from her. Afraid that Bubby might somehow influence me to become religious, my mother discouraged our relationship, even thwarting my plans to visit her. But I found ways to get around that.

By the time I was eleven, I would play hooky from school and take a bus from my house all the way to the neighborhood on the other side of Haifa where my Bubby lived. She was always thrilled to see me. She never asked, "Does *Imma* know you're here?" or "How is it you don't have to be in school today?" A sixth sense must have told her the truth, but she cherished my visits too much to blow the whistle on me. She won my heart for that.

She and my mother only partly reconciled before Bubby passed away when I was fifteen. Shortly afterward, we moved to America. It was a temporary move for my parents—my father was soon called back to Israel by his employer. My younger sister returned with them, but I was in college then, and engaged to my husband, Len. The future I dreamed of was not in Israel.

Fast forward about 40 years. During that time, four life-and-death emergencies brought me flying across oceans to my mother's hospital bedside. I have learned to dread the sound of a phone ringing in the middle of the night: Who calls in the wee hours of the morning with anything but bad news?

This time it was a man's voice, speaking in Hebrew, muffled by static. "Yael, this is your Uncle Avrohom. I'm sorry to give you bad news, but your mother is very ill. The doctors say there is no time to lose… Come immediately if you want to see her once more."

On the plane to Israel, I calmed my taut nerves by reminding myself that my mother had survived medical crises before. She'd outlived bleak prognostications, always drawing on the will to live that had been so tested during the Holocaust.

Uncle Avrohom, Mother's *Chareidi* brother, knew this better than I. Although my mother kept him at arm's distance all the years, he was the one she listed as "next of kin" in her hospital records. He responded to every emergency call, just as if they were close.

Uncle Avrohom's daughter met me at the airport, a somber look in her eyes. "How bad is it?" I wanted to ask, but I just stared at her.

"Your mother is in a coma," my cousin told me gently. I expected to hear worse.

"Is there any hope …?

She cast her eyes downward. "My father said *Shema Yisrael* with her a little while ago."

Although I spoke a fluent Hebrew, I did not know the precise significance of these two Hebrew words, *Shema Yisrael*, spoken at a sick person's bedside. But I could guess. My heart plummeted.

I approached Mother's bedside. I leaned over and kissed her cheek. Tears spilled down my cheek onto hers. Was I imagining that her eyelids fluttered? Suddenly those deep brown eyes opened and gazed into mine. "I'm thirsty," she whispered.

The most hard-boiled doctors and nurses on the floor were

dumbfounded at this medical reversal. As she slowly recovered her health, this miracle led to another: In a private moment, *Imma* told Avrohom, that she knew that his prayers at her bedside saved her from death. He then told her that hundreds of yeshivah students in Jerusalem, adults and children, were all praying for the recovery of Leba Mindel bat Leah.

"I think…it is time, maybe, to listen *tzu der Mama*," my mother whispered, lapsing into Yiddish, which astonished me. She wanted to talk to Uncle Avrohom about koshering her kitchen, about observing Shabbat. Tears came to my uncle's eyes.

The bittersweet element in this strange development was that my mother let me know that she would be pleased if I would also begin to do these things. She did not understand that while she had something to return to—the religious upbringing of her childhood years—all I had was the aversion to religious dogma that she herself had instilled in me. My husband's parents were second-generation Reform Jews. No legacy to hold onto there either.

I had raised my two daughters – now married adults—as I had been raised, in a totally secular environment. The only difference was that I'd had a Bubby through whose eyes I had glimpsed a universe that lay beyond my reach. My girls had no such connection and weren't looking for one.

Or so I thought.

Connections, I soon discovered, can come when you least expect them, seemingly from nowhere. In my daughter Carol's case, it was the pain of not having children that created a connection with Judaism. After five years of childlessness, she felt desperate. She was about to start infertility treatments and was considering taking a controversial hormonal drug. Her husband wanted her to postpone these steps until they had settled in their new home in Marlboro, New Jersey.

Something unexpected happened there. They met a young rabbi

who introduced them to the world of Torah, a world of which they both knew nothing. He gave classes on the meaning of the Jewish holidays and fundamental Jewish concepts. I watched in amazement as Carol and her husband became more and more interested in Jewish tradition.

The rabbi brought them to a Gateways weekend seminar. It sounds melodramatic to say this, but something happened that weekend that changed their lives. Carol met an instructor at the seminar who gave classes on the role of women in Judaism. She urged Carol not to go forward with invasive procedures or hormone therapy until she first tried a potent "treatment" that had absolutely no side effects. It was called the "laws of family purity." Carol sat through an introduction to this guide to a Jewish marriage.

"It moved me to tears," she told me afterward. "Something inside me feels deeply in sync with this. Somehow, I know Michael and I must have a truly Jewish marriage. We're going to try this."

Carol cancelled her appointments with her doctors and she and her husband made a commitment to study and keep the laws of family purity. Nine and a half months later, Carol gave birth to baby boy. At the *Brit*, I thought my heart would burst, sharing the intense joy that this tiny child brought his parents. I felt the pull of generations. I knew there had been a miracle within a miracle.

Carol and Michael were now Sabbath observant and strictly kosher. To make it easy for them to spend time with us, Len and I decided to *kasher* our home, too. But keeping Shabbat was a different story. Both of us worked at jobs that did the greatest volume of business on Saturday. I was a sales manager in a department store; he sold jewelry to retailers, requiring a lot of weekend traveling. There was no way we could keep our jobs if we kept Shabbat. It was out of the question. The price was too high.

The only discomfort we had with this position is that Carol and Michael had been faced with the same dilemma and had said "yes" where we said "no." They had just taken out a mortgage and had just had a baby—yet Michael went ahead and quit a job with real potential. Len told me he thought they had made a big mistake. "They're not living in the real world," he said.

But I was starting to like their world. They were part of a small growing community of Orthodox Jews that included beginners and "old-timers" and exuded a warm sense of family and belonging. We found that same warmth and camaraderie at the Gateways seminar that Len and I finally attended, urged on by Carol and Michael who pleaded with us to join them.

With my command of Hebrew, I had an edge over some of the other participants. I found the classes on the mystical meaning of the Hebrew alphabet deeply inspiring. Len was fascinated by the lectures showing how the Torah's laws of kosher slaughter revealed an astounding grasp of anatomy that could not possibly have been known by people in ancient times.

A strange thing happened at the conclusion of one of the lectures. The speaker finished his talk with a ringing plea to everyone to take advantage of Jewish educational opportunities.

"At the very least, deepen your sense of Jewish identity and Jewish pride," he said. "Know what it means to live as a Jew." He concluded with the words *Shema Yisrael*, the very words I remembered my Uncle Avrohom reciting when my mother lay on her deathbed. I trembled, recalling how my mother had miraculously come back to life after the doctors had written her off.

Living as a Jew, dying as a Jew... To die as one, you had to live as one. My mother, redeemed from the clutches of death, had finally grasped that. What would it take for her daughter to see the truth?

Three years after sharing their story, Yael and Len are in a very different place, literally and spiritually. They sold their home and moved to the religious community outside Lakewood to which Carol and Michael belonged. After Yael resigned from her job, she and Len became fully Sabbath observant and she found a new job as a librarian. Len had a more difficult time finding work, but eventually launched a new business.

These were not easy changes for the couple. In addition to leaving behind their social network, they had to adjust their standard of living to a lowered income and tighter budget. Yael says there were moments when they wondered if they had made a mistake.

But with time, she says, they've come to see that the sacrifices have been worth it. Their nurturing community, their wonderful new friends and the joy of being close to their children and grandchildren make their lives very full. "Some days I even have a glimpse of that wonderful sublime thing called 'pure faith,' commented Yael. "These are the moments that money can't buy."

It Takes
a Child

Brenda's Story

Growing up in Queens, my siblings and I all wished we were at least second-generation American like our neighbors and friends. We loved our parents, but our mother's Israeli accent embarrassed us; and the way Dad stuck out as a foreigner—a Jew born in Iraq—made my brothers uncomfortable.

It was an Italian neighborhood so, of course, we had Italian friends. My father would grumble under his breath, "Why don't you have any Jewish friends?" That was typical of his confused way of raising us. After all, what choices did we have, living where we lived and going to the local schools?

Tradition was important to my father, but he wanted to pass it down by rote, without rhyme or reason. He either didn't know or chose not to explain what was behind the Jewish rituals he wanted us to keep. That made my brothers and me rebel behind his back. Why on earth did we need to keep kosher when all our friends could eat out at the corner pizza parlor? What use did we have for going to synagogue when we could barely read Hebrew, couldn't follow the services, and were bored out of our minds?

I have a feeling that my father would have sent us kids to Jewish schools if he could have afforded it. But the shortage of money, and the fact that our mother was not in favor of it, ruled out Jewish schools.

To accommodate Dad, we had two sets of dishes, for milk and meat. But to accommodate Mom, we ate non-kosher food on them! Because my father insisted on it, we kept Passover. We went without bread, and took the toaster down to the basement. But since my mother knew so little about how to observe the holiday, 99% of what we ate during the holiday was almost certainly forbidden.

There was no Shabbos in my home because my father felt he had no choice but to go to work on Saturday in order to support his family. It was only at the end of his life, when he was too old and weak to continue working, that he began to observe Orthodox rituals as he had done as a boy in Baghdad. By then, Mom had passed away, and my brothers and I were all married—to non-Jews.

Every one of those marriages was a blow to my father. The idea that from his six children he would have no Jewish grandchildren was a source of anguish. It was only later in life that I understood his pain. He railed at us for deserting our faith, but I saw nothing wrong with marrying a Christian. My brothers and I were not interested in perpetuating my parents' weird blend of Israeli-Sephardic Jewish tradition and culture. We wanted to be all-American kids, free of our parents' baggage.

To give you an idea of the "dual personality" of our home, my father made all of us say *Shema Yisrael* when we went to sleep at night. Even though we understood not a word of it, and were completely ignorant of any other prayers in our Jewish tradition, my brothers and I were expected to say this prayer every single night at bedtime. (When I grew up and was already living on my own, this practice stayed with me. Somehow, it had gotten under my skin and I couldn't ditch it, even after my marriage to a non-Jew.)

It was only as I grew older that I realized how my father's brand of Judaism reflected his own conflicts about his heritage. He was already very old when he told me the details of how his father had died. Until then, all I knew was that my grandfather had been killed in an anti-Semitic disturbance in Baghdad in the 1930s. Now I found out how. He had been dragged off a bus by Jew-hating thugs and beaten to death.

Terrified for his life, my father, who was then in his teens, had fled with his family to Israel. In the scrambling around for means to support the family, he and his brothers abandoned their religious lifestyle. They gradually adopted the secular values of their new homeland. The next generation was much further removed from the old ways. None of my Israeli cousins on my father's side are religious today.

The pattern of each generation drifting farther away from Judaism was unexpectedly broken with my daughter, Shari. When she was only ten years old, she decided to keep Shabbos.

I was divorced by then, and it was just the two of us. When she was four, the public school kindergarten I had chosen for her was already full when I went to apply. The Jewish day school was close by and had an excellent pre-school program. I signed her up, thinking it would be for just one year.

But Shari blossomed there, and loved everything she encountered, from the little friends she made, to the *parshah* stories, to the Yom Tov songs and the arts and crafts she brought home. I was so happy for her. I didn't foresee the dilemma that lay ahead until it was too late.

One Saturday, when Shari was eleven, I planned a family outing at the beach with a bunch of Shari's cousins, aunts, and uncles. Shari had been observing Shabbos for several months at home. When plans for the trip came up and her cousins urged her to come along, she was very torn. Finally, at my prodding, she relented and said she would come. At the last minute, though, five minutes before our ride came, she had a change of heart.

"I can't go. I can't go into a car on Shabbos," she cried.

I said it was too late for me to cancel, everyone was counting on our being there, and that I couldn't let them down. I said she could stay home if she wanted. She agonized over it until my brother and sister-in-law arrived with the kids and I started loading the picnic things inside their car. At the last minute, biting her lip, she climbed into the back seat with her cousins.

But it was pure torment for her. She cried at the beach and wouldn't go into the water. She just lay on her towel in the sand, miserable and full of guilt, not talking to anyone. I thought to myself, "What am I doing to this child? Whether it's right or wrong, true or false, how can I force her to go against her conscience?" I promised myself I would never again put her into this position.

A couple of weeks later, Shari and I went to our first Gateways seminar. It had been billed as a four-day exploration of Judaism with first-class hotel accommodations and a fantastic children's program. I was on my guard, knowing that the rabbis running the program would be giving us an Orthodox slant on everything.

But I quickly got over my reservations. The rapport, the meals, and the good feeling in the air alone would have made it worth the money. But what happened there went beyond good company and fabulous food. It was like watching a very blurry picture come slowly into focus. It was like standing on a mountaintop for the first time, getting a full sweep of the region near your home far below.

All my life I had kept bits and pieces of Judaism like random pieces of silverware that don't match up. The Judaism I grew up with was so arbitrary and confusing I never had the patience to learn anything about it. Now, I began to see where Jewish laws and rituals fit into a grand scheme, and some of the reasons behind them.

I learned that Jews throughout the ages, for over 3,000 years, had been practicing—and still practiced—the Torah's laws in the exact same way, with all its myriad details. As the rabbi put it, my grandfather from Baghdad could trade "identity cards" with a Jew from halfway around the world—or even from a different century—and they would immediately recognize each other as brothers.

Their Judaism was not a mixed-up hodge-podge like the one I inherited from my father, but an orderly system built into day to-day living. It's a system that is portable, from one country to another, across oceans and mountains and major cataclysms, across centuries, right into today's world.

My grandfather in Baghdad, like his grandfather before him and all the way up the chain of generations, had celebrated Passover as a prime opportunity to pass down a precious heritage from father to son: not nostalgic mementos of the long-lost world or bits and pieces of a broken tradition, but a vibrant, hands-on legacy.

To hear Rabbi Ordman conclude one of his lectures with the one line of the Bible I knew in Hebrew—*Shema Yisrael*—astounded me. But it was learning that these particular words are so central and holy to Judaism that brought tears to my eyes. Could it be that these very words I whispered every night—without any clue to what they meant—had helped me through so many difficult times in my life?

Sometimes it takes a child to make you see straight. It was Shari's embrace of Judaism that slowly opened my heart to it. In fact, her innocent belief in a soul existing before life kindled my own belief.

When she was only four, she said to me, "You're my mommy, because before I was born, I picked you." A few years later, when she was old enough to know why her family was so small—just the two of us—and old enough to feel the loneliness of it, she said something like that again. This time it was during one of those moments when life seems so heavy you have to fight to get out of bed in the morning.

"Mommy, you know something," she said. "Before I was born, I picked you. Even though I knew you would get divorced and I wouldn't have a father, I picked you to be my mother."

My eyes stung. I don't imagine getting picked for anything in the world—even president of the United States—can be as glorious as getting picked as best-mother-in-the-world by your own child. But beyond the emotional high it gave me was the sense that there was much more here than a child's way of saying, "I love you, Mommy." There was something profoundly moving about her certainty that her soul existed even before her birth.

When I think about my family's history, without belief in a

Jewish soul, there is no other way to explain the miracle of a child like Shari. Think of the bizarre pattern. My grandfather was killed by Jew-haters. In reaction, his children fled from their homeland and, in the end, rejected their religion and heritage. His grandchildren were almost completely assimilated and most of *their* children were not even Jewish.

Given this situation, what are the odds of a young child in this estranged clan reversing history and embracing Judaism? How did such a thing happen?

It comforts me to think that perhaps it was because G–d had pity on my grandfather's soul and sent Shari to this world so that my grandfather's life and death would not be in vain. So that at least one link in a family chain stretching back for so many centuries would survive the storms and begin to turn back the tide.

Create For Me a Pure Heart

Daphne's Story

My father was the child of Holocaust survivors who raised their only child without any connection to Judaism. As a boy, he knew nothing of Shabbos, Jewish holidays or *kashrus*. Even the name his parents gave him—Christopher—seemed to be an effort to keep him at a safe distance from the world in which they had been raised. No future onslaught against Jews would threaten this beloved son.

I was very attached to him, even though my parents were divorced and I lived with my mother. Dad was a renowned orthopedic surgeon—high-powered, brilliant, and very driven. I had to use all my wits to try to carve a niche for myself in his frenzied schedule. It was like chasing the wind.

I became religious in college, with the help of some close friends. My mother was very supportive, and I shared with her a lot of what I was going through. For me, *Yiddishkeit* had an immediate sense of *click!*—a key fitting right into a lock. Friends would take me along with them to eat Shabbos meals at peoples' homes, and I saw how Shabbos linked families together in a beautiful way.

I got to know some wonderful people and eventually felt like one of the family when I visited them. I was fascinated by their family interactions, by the closeness and warmth, even when the kids were bickering or there was tension in the air.

I began to devise ways of interesting my father in Judaism. I knew he'd be impressed by a religion that was both ancient and contemporary all at once. That's how we ended up together at a Gateways seminar last year, a small miracle in itself.

Dad wasn't really interested in going with me. He consented because he happened to need a vacation and he saw how deeply I wanted him to come.

"Are you on a religious binge or something?" he challenged me. I sidestepped the question.

"Dad, trust me, it'll be meaningful. You'll be glad you went," I told him.

But would he be? What did I really know about my father's feelings about G–d, religion…immortality? Those subjects were not table-talk in our home. Deep down, I wanted him to come, because even if he didn't pick up an interest in Judaism, he would at least have a deeper appreciation of what had become a very important part of my life. I had been making my own decisions for years, but I still hungered to have his vote of confidence.

It was a beautiful weekend. I felt fortunate that we had been placed for the Shabbos meals at the table of some of the most cordial and interesting people on the Gateways staff. They had come with some of their children—little ones and teenagers—and it was just the kind of Shabbos table I wanted my father to experience.

He actually attended all the lectures, without that foot-tapping impatience I know so well. One of the speakers tied in the miracle of Jewish survival through centuries of persecution with the system of religious transmission that has kept Torah alive for hundreds of generations. He showed how many of the Torah's laws are Judaism's built-in system of preserving the memory of how the Jewish people came to be G–d's chosen nation.

The fascinating part to this lecture was the way the model of Holocaust remembrance demonstrated the difficulty of preserving historical truth, even of the most globally renowned event. Only 60 years after World War II, an entire industry of Holocaust-denial literature has sprung up. In the face of the human tendency to deny and forget, how could survivors ensure that the Holocaust would never be forgotten?

By the same token, the speaker asked, how could G–d ensure

that the Jewish people would never forget their experience of slavery and miraculous redemption?

I stole a look at my father. His expression was pensive and it seemed to me, sad. I knew the parallel with Holocaust remembrance had touched a nerve somewhere. My grandparents had chosen to keep both their war memories *and* their Jewish identity tightly locked away. They had left behind so little for their son to hold on to, so little to pass on to the next generation.

At the end of the weekend, my father was in a strangely subdued mood. I gathered my courage and finally told him of my plans to leave for Israel at the end of the month, to study at a seminary for a year. He didn't raise any of the objections about career and livelihood that I expected from him. Instead, he said simply, "Daphne, I think I understand what you're doing. You're making a fine choice."

I flew to Israel with those wonderful words of blessing. A few months after I arrived, I was in a bookstore in Geulah. On an impulse, I bought Dad a beautiful edition of ArtScroll's Stone Chumash and mailed it to him, allowing myself to fantasize that he would be enthralled by it, that it would be a stepping-stone to a spiritual journey.

I had been in Israel for about four months when I received a shattering phone-call from my brother in the States. Dad had suffered a massive stroke and was barely hanging on to life. He suffered multiple organ failure and was on life support. They had to shock his heart several times to get it going. I was advised to come home before it was too late. The call came just two hours before Sukkos.

As terrified as I was, I felt that those two days of Yom Tov in Jerusalem were a gift. I ran to the Kotel to pray, I said Tehillim and cried my heart out, asking G–d for a miracle.

After the holiday, I took the first flight back to New York. As much as I had prepared myself, seeing my Dad on a respirator was devastating. He looked pale and drawn, his life slipping away by the second. The doctors were giving him less than a 50-50 chance.

Though he was unconscious, I spent a month in the ICU, praying by his side. When he finally opened his eyes, he was so swollen that he couldn't talk or move a finger. But he had passed the critical point!

Very, very slowly, he began to recover. When they finally transferred him out of the ICU, one of the nurses was wiping her eyes. "Most people in his condition never make it out of here alive," she told me. "Your father had a miracle."

While Dad was still unconscious, the doctors warned me that even if he pulled out of the danger zone, the neurological damage could be very severe. When his vital signs became stronger, but he couldn't stay awake or utter a word, I had a cold fear that I might never have my father back again, even if he did survive.

It was months before he was able to communicate. Gradually, as the swelling went down, he recognized his family and showed signs that his mental faculties were intact. He was admitted to a rehabilitation floor; over many long months, he regained the ability to feed himself and to walk with a walker.

There are miracles within miracles. While there was no neurological damage as the doctors had feared, something about my father was so changed, it was almost as though he'd become a different person.

He had always had an impatient nature; he was used to giving orders and having them carried out immediately. When you were talking to him, he had a way of glancing at his watch that made you feel dismissed. He'd nod perfunctorily and you knew he wasn't following you. Or he'd cut you off in the middle with a comment or question that put an end to the conversation. That impatience should have discouraged the Gateways people from contacting him after the seminar he and I attended.

But it didn't. Staff members called him a number of times to check if he had any interest in attending a class or setting up a home or office study. He kept giving them a brush-off. "Call me another time," he would mutter, "I'm very tied up right now."

Gateways must have sensed there was a genuine spark of interest under the brusqueness. In any case, one of the callers kept trying to reach him. After learning about his stroke, this man waited many weeks until Dad had regained some strength. Finally, he called just to say that he was *davening* for Dad's recovery. After that, he'd call once a week to say hello and offer a few words of encouragement.

My father was touched by this man's caring. About a month later, they had their first learning session over the phone.

I had an occasion to speak to my dad's new *chavrusah* soon afterward. He told me how well the session had gone, and of my father's intelligent comments. They had discussed the creation of the world and its implications that the world has a Master. The man used words like "gentle" and "sweet" in describing my father. Six months ago, had someone described him in these incongruous terms, I would have laughed. But I didn't now. Somehow, the stroke had altered my father's personality, tempering his "drill sergeant" disposition to a mildness and sweetness we never knew was there.

One day last week, I called him and my aunt picked up the phone. "Daphne, you called at just the right time. Your father is awake. He just settled himself into his chair with his favorite book."

"Which one is that?" I asked.

"You know, that big blue book you sent him from Israel. He has his nose in it all the time."

The big blue book! I pictured the Chumash that had lain untouched on Dad's shelf for so many months, with my dream and prayer wrapped inside. I thought of this book and its holy contents waiting patiently as a life-and-death drama played out and an ailing heart was granted a second chance. Tears came to my eyes as I thought of my father as a new man in more ways than one, and prayed that the words of the Torah might finally take root in his healing heart.

A Gift from Dakota

Mike's Story

About five years ago, I joined a Native American spirituality group that has a very old tradition in the Northern Great Plains and the Rocky Mountains. Feeling an affinity for their lifestyle, I made my mind up to "commit"—the term they used for a formal conversion.

But the head of the group, a Native American named Nick Dakota, took me aside and said, "Michael, if you really want to travel this road, I'll help you. But I wonder if you know that as a Jew, you come from one of the greatest spiritual traditions in humanity. Maybe you ought to find out more about your own roots before taking this step."

I can't tell you how surprised I was to hear that from him. I thought, what could he possibly know about Judaism that I didn't know? Whatever I knew—which was based on the few weeks of bar mitzvah lessons my parents forced on me when I was thirteen—hardly inspired love or respect. My father had to bribe me with big bucks to get me to perform for that bar mitzvah. There wasn't even a pretense about it being anything but an empty extravaganza.

Was this the "spiritual tradition" Dakota was talking about?

"Judaism interests me about as much as Christianity," I told him, holding up my thumb and forefinger in a zero.

"You're sure you're not confusing the two? They're actually quite different."

"Yeah, I know," I said, even though when it came down to it, I didn't. What was so different? They were both just shams, as far as I was concerned.

"Someone with Jewish ancestors is connected to a very different spiritual source than someone with Christian ancestors," he countered. "To sever your connection with that source is...well, I'd say you'd need a pretty strong reason for doing that."

He looked me straight in the eye. I had the feeling he knew that when it came to Judaism, my mental file was completely blank. It was embarrassing. I ended up pushing off the "commitment" exercise and soon after that, I left the commune.

Partly I was miffed that they weren't welcoming me with open arms. And I was rankled by Dakota's comments about my Jewish ancestors. If my ancestors needed an Indian from the Great Plains to be concerned about keeping their Jewish line going, what did that say about me, their descendant, who was ready to walk away without an ounce of regret?

For a year or more, I drifted around southern California, linking up with friends and trying different things. I went back to school for a while but began to feel that my spiritual quest was leading me in circles. I thought about heading back east, but what would I be returning to? A job? A relationship? A life? None of the above. I was only twenty, but I was burned out.

"Check out your people's roots." Dakota's words echoed in my mind. As I boarded the plane, I had the bleak thought that if nothing else, New York certainly has a lot of Jews to offer, and some were bound to have roots. How deep would I have to dig?

I moved back home with my parents while trying to re-orient myself to life in the Big Apple. Someone told me about the Jewish Enrichment Center in Manhattan. I began showing up at some classes and social activities sponsored by the group. Several months later, I attended my first Gateways seminar.

It was a disaster.

I had discovered that there are spiritual aspects of Judaism—belief in a soul, and life after death – and I began to take an interest in them. I had even begun to observe some of the rituals connected with Shabbos and Jewish holidays. But it was all on a strictly emotional level. It didn't have anything to do with "absolute truth." I didn't believe in that. My philosophy was whatever works for you is right for you.

So here come these Gateways rabbis, and for them, "absolute truth" is exactly what Judaism is all about! Even though it was clear that I wasn't expected to do anything "religious" during the seminar, the very presence of these rabbis and their families made me feel hemmed in.

My initial negative reaction colored everything I heard at the classes. As one speaker was explaining the devious tactics some missionaries use to "ensnare" Jews, I kept thinking, "He just can't bear to have a person exposed to any belief but his own brand of truth!"

Another speaker addressed the Israeli-Palestinian conflict. Someone commented that the Israeli occupation was immoral, and that a two-state solution was the only way to end the conflict. The speaker shot back that the West Bank was indeed *"owner-occupied,"* and until the Arabs prove capable of reining in terrorism, it would be suicidal for Israel to grant them a state. I almost groaned aloud. Where I come from, that's flat-out racism.

I had to admit that the rabbis were intelligent and well-informed. In addition to their knowledge of Judaism, they had a broad grasp of history and other disciplines. But their politics were so right-wing! And they were anti-pluralist and deeply conservative. We came from different worlds.

Back home, I grappled with their concept that it isn't possible to reach a lofty spiritual state without physical actions like *tzitzit, tefillin,* and *kashrut.* I was much more interested in meditation and mysticism. And yet, the more I thought about it, the more I saw the point that Judaism without the *mitzvot* wouldn't be much different from Christianity, if you put aside belief in J.C.

It made sense that without keeping the Torah, being Jewish has nowhere to go. You might as well be a non-Jew. My parents and the Jewish society I was raised in believed that they were "good Jews," without practicing what they regarded as antiquated laws and rituals. What did that mean? How was that different from simply being good people?

Historians and philosophers talk about the "Judeo-Christian tradition." But I learned in my classes that Christianity came on the scene a thousand years after Judaism was an established religion. I knew Judaism pre-dated Christianity, *but a thousand years*! Christianity helped itself to Jewish ethics, while ditching the commandments.

Dakota's words came back to me: "…as a Jew you come from one of the most spiritual traditions in the history of humanity…" He would have loved these rabbis. I almost wished I could speak to him and let him know how much he had complicated my life by closing the door in my face.

After the seminar, the Gateways staff called me a several times to ask if I was interested in exploring some aspect of Judaism with a class or a learning partner. I began taking classes with Rabbi Becher, a senior lecturers at Gateways who came to the Jewish Enrichment Center once a week. A half a year later, I was running into conflicts with my family by starting in earnest to keep *kashrut* and Shabbat.

It threw everyone in the family off balance. My dad took me aside one day and said, "Mike, what's gotten into you? Not taking phone calls on Saturday, lying in your room in the dark, keeping dietary laws? This is fanatical. This is just not our way."

"I can move out," I offered.

"That's not the point. I'm worried about you. You used to be a person who valued intellectual freedom. How did you get sucked into all this?"

My two older brothers got in the act and we had some intense discussions—well, shouting matches—about Judaism. I decided to move out before we all killed each other, and I found an apartment on the West Side. Then something completely unexpected happened.

My aunt Sylvia, Mom's oldest sister, passed away and in her will she asked that my great-grandmother's silver candelabra, a family heirloom which had been sent to her over 50 years ago from Poland, be given to me. Her daughters were surprised. Even though, like their mother, they were not religious and had never lit Shabbat candles, they assumed that such a valuable keepsake would be left to them.

My "flipping out" and becoming Shabbat-observant had become well known in the family while Aunt Sylvia was still alive. She had been impatient with me for indulging in "foolishness." Strangely, though, when it came time for her to decide to whom she would entrust her cherished heirloom, her Shabbat-observing nephew no longer seemed quite so foolish.

I took the candlesticks, had them polished and restored, and began to light them every Friday before sundown. When I came home for a visit, I brought them along. They were ancient-looking and out of place in our modern-style living room. Surprisingly, nobody said a word about that. Those ancient candlesticks seemed to command respect.

I found some old photos of my great-grandparents and a memorial book about the town of Yaslow in Poland, just a few miles from Auschwitz, where my mother's grandparents and extended family had lived until the Holocaust. Almost all of them were murdered. Looking at my great-grandfather's picture, I tried to read his expression. He had that severe pose typical of old photographs, but his eyes were soft and kind, sort of looking off sadly into the future. The long beard and side curls that once would have scared me off, seemed to give him a distinguished, righteous look.

I wondered what he would tell me if he saw me today. We often say, "Get a life." I imagined my great-grandfather telling me, "Get a Jewish life."

About a year after the first one, I went to my second Gateways seminar. I was wary, remembering how turned off I had been. But I was amazed at how different this experience was. They had really made changes. The atmosphere was much friendlier and more open-minded, and the religious contingent was less overpowering. I complimented Rabbi Jordan, one of the coordinators, for having made so many accommodations, and he looked at me, surprised.

"Actually, Mike, we've kept pretty much the same format since you were here last. The staff's mostly the same, too."

"Well, it sure seems a whole lot different."

He laughed. "Think it might be *you* that's changed?"

I thought about that. He was right. I was less defensive. I wasn't as afraid of the dire implications of "absolutes"—absolute truth, absolute right and wrong. I actually found myself dreaming up schemes to get my brothers and my parents to come to a seminar. I knew it would be a strong experience for them.

For some time, I had been considering quitting my job and going for a year to Israel to learn in a yeshivah. I'd spoken about it to one of the rabbis at Gateways, but for one reason or another, the plan never got off the ground. That weekend, I found myself pressed to the wall on the subject. It was late at night, after the *melaveh malkah*, and Rabbi Greenblatt kind of pigeonholed me. He asked me what kind of motivation would galvanize me to take off time to learn in a yeshivah. He said he could see I'd progressed in my Jewish observance but had reached a plateau. I wasn't moving ahead.

We talked about that. I realized I'd been throwing up all kinds of roadblocks over the past year. Once, quitting my job and flying off to

Israel was the type of thing I could do in the blink of an eye. Adventure was my elixir. But now I balked. Who knows what kind of major upheaval I'd be setting myself up for?

"I just made arrangements for a young man to go to a yeshivah in Jerusalem in a few weeks," Rabbi Greenblatt offered. "How about letting me make you a reservation, too, Mike?" I wanted to say, "Sure, go ahead," but I couldn't get out the words. For some reason, I almost felt like crying. Straddling the fence like this was driving me crazy. "I'm too tied up now. Try me in a few months," I finally mumbled.

A few weeks later, something happened at work that showed me how the Man Above really pulls the strings. One of the executives from our Paris branch came to visit our office. The guy looks me up and down, gesturing disdainfully at my *tzitzit*. In his French-accented English, he snorts, "Mr. Weiner, those Jew-strings under your shirt: they will have to go."

"I'm not sure I understand you," I answer without blinking.

Frenchie may be used to sneering at Jews in his anti-Semitic homeland, but in America that kind of behavior from an employer is not just politically incorrect; it can land you in court with a lawsuit.

"Are you saying you want me to tuck them in when I visit a client?"

"I'm saying get rid of them! Next, we will have Chinese workers coming in with Chinese attire and Indians with their native dress and who knows what else. This is a business, not a circus."

I was so furious I wanted to knock this guy out, but I stayed cool. Suddenly I realized that I wanted them to fire me. And I wanted it to happen over the issue of my *tzitzit*. So I calmly turned my back on the guy and went back to what I was doing. The temperature in the room dropped to below zero. I could feel Frenchie glaring at me, but I ignored him. He stomped out.

Before the week was out, they gave me my "walking papers," with some severance pay thrown in. Instead of arguing or threatening to sue for religious discrimination, as they might have expected, I was exulting. I actually went over to the head honchos and thanked them. They acted flustered and mumbled some awkward nonsense. I cleared out my desk, wished everyone good luck and waved goodbye, almost doing a little jig out the door. I couldn't wait to phone Rabbi Greenblatt.

Frenchie no doubt thinks he scored a big one against a Jew. He doesn't even know what a pawn he's been. He just handed this Jew a ticket to Jerusalem—and the best possible chance of finally "getting a life."

Special thanks to Mike for granting an interview in the midst of last-minute packing, just two days before he boarded a plane for Israel. He is now studying in a yeshivah in Har Nof.

Planting
In Tears

Betty's Story

I was one of barely a handful of Jews in my Wilmington, Delaware high school, and like the others, made it a point to be inconspicuous. Then an incident in the tenth grade changed my life.

My history teacher was telling the class about a certain Jewish pilot who distinguished himself in World War II, and despite the anti-Semitism in his country's air force, was presented with the highest medal for bravery. The teacher suddenly turned to me and asked me if perhaps I was related to that Jewish pilot, since our last names were the same.

From that moment on, I was branded.

I was shoved and tripped in the hallway and on the school bus. The toughest troublemakers in the school would pull my books from my arms and throw them down, laughing in my face. Swastikas were scrawled on my locker. I learned about the many foul-mouthed names for Jews in the English language. I learned what it means to be hated for no reason other than your faith.

I was too frightened of retaliation to complain to the teachers or principal. I tried to save myself by running or ducking out of the way whenever I could, and by faking illness so I wouldn't have to go to school. Sometimes I was forced to fight back, but I always lost. Life was torture. From then on, I dreamed of going to Israel. I thought of it as a magical place, a safe haven from anti-Semites, a place where I would actually feel a sense of belonging.

The terrible irony is that I had almost zero connection with the Jewish faith. My foster parents were Christians and had taught me that I could be a Christian, too, even while being a Jew. So I went to church with them, took Bible classes and did everything a Christian does—with one exception: I never consented to being baptized.

A few times, the baptism ceremony was set up and I told everyone that *this time* I would finally go through with it, but at the last minute, I'd always balk. Somehow I felt that the part of me that was Jewish would be totally erased if I were baptized. That would be the ultimate renunciation of all I had from my Jewish parents.

I had been in foster care from the age of seven. I never knew my father, and my mother lived two thousand miles away. We almost never saw one another and had very little contact by phone. But my father's sister lived on the other side of town and would call me from time to time.

One day, when I was about fifteen, she told me, "Betty, this Christian-Jewish business has to stop. You can't be both. Make up your mind."

"But Mom and Dad told me —" I tried to explain but she cut me off.

"They told you what the Church says. But I'm here to tell you that according to Judaism, you're a Jew. I know I'm no authority," she said, "and there are lots of things about Judaism I don't observe. But one thing I'm absolutely sure of is this: you can't be a Jew and worship like a Christian!"

When I became victimized at school for being Jewish, it was right after my aunt had given me notice that I was living a lie. Without her ultimatum, "Make up your mind!" I might have fought off everyone's accusations and turned myself into a Christian, at least in the eyes of the world. But her words goaded me in the other direction. I thought—if I have to suffer this hate, let it at least be for a purpose.

But as the harassment continued, I became more and more desperate. Finally, at the end of 11th grade, I snapped. I cried hysterically at home and for the first time, filled my foster parents in on all that was going on. I said that if they made me go back to school, I'd kill myself.

At first they thought I was exaggerating or somehow responsible for bringing trouble on myself. I gave them details and they started to realize that this madness came from kids who were simply evil. They switched me to a different high school a few counties away where there were more Jews. It was like being let out of prison. I finally could focus on learning and living a normal life like other kids my age.

I was nineteen when I walked into a synagogue for the first time. I was going to college in Boston and some friends had steered me to this place for Rosh Hashanah. It was a *shul* that kept a row of seats in the back that were free of charge for people who couldn't afford to pay. I didn't know my way around the prayer book, and I'm sure I looked it. Several women there were very kind and encouraging to me, showing me the place from time to time. I relaxed and stopped feeling like an intruder.

Still, it was all so alien: the separation of men and women, nothing in English, no sermon, all this emotional singing followed by total pin-drop quiet. What was going on? I was so bewildered.

But I came back for the rest of the holidays. By then, I had become more familiar with the routines and some of the women invited me for meals. Through some of the people I met there, I was introduced to a local Jewish outreach organization that offered weekly classes on many different topics in Judaism.

That winter, I got a call from a friend of mine, Robyn Fischer, who had moved to New York where she had begun working for Gateways. Robyn wanted me to experience a seminar. "You'll love the classes," she promised. I trusted her intuition but couldn't afford the price. A true friend, she arranged a subsidy for me.

It wasn't just the classes I enjoyed at the seminar. I appreciated the freedom to ask questions about anything at all. "That's a great question," the rabbi would say encouragingly, no matter how dumb it sounded to my ears. Another unusual thing about this weekend was that the usual barriers you feel with strangers didn't exist here. I made so many new connections with people. Parting from these new friends – Jewish friends—at the end of the week left me with a wistful feeling. I didn't want this encounter to end.

Returning home, I wondered how I could fit more learning into my life. I felt impatient to get past the "ignorant beginner" stage.

Then came a phone call that hit me like a bombshell. A woman I had been in touch with once or twice after the seminar called. "Betty? This is Leah from Gateways. I've got wonderful news for you. We're sending you to Israel!"

I laughed in disbelief. The only thing I had ever won before was a set of coffee mugs. "I think you have the wrong Betty," I said. "This is Betty Gordon."

"I know this is Betty Gordon…" She was laughing with me. "Betty, are you there? Okay, here's the story. We know you'd love the chance to study in Israel and we'd like to help you. Rabbi Moskowitz pulled a few strings and we have special funding for such a project. All you have to do is fill out the seminary application …"

I was speechless. It had to be some kind of mistake. "Would you like to speak to him?" Leah continued. "He'll give you the details."

I had met Rabbi Eli Moskowitz at the seminar just a few weeks earlier. I was browsing through the books and tapes on Judaism that were out on display, and had no idea what to choose. I turned for some guidance to the first person around me who seemed to be knowledgeable. It was Rabbi Moskowitz. In just a few seconds, he seemed to grasp what I needed. He pointed out a few books that he said I would find very useful.

Now he was on the phone. "Betty, the offer is absolutely legit. I hope you'll take us up on it."

Tears came to my eyes. "But you hardly know me."

"We know a good investment when we see one."

He spoke to me about a Torah school for women that he felt was perfect for me. I was in my second year of college; the thought of taking off a year not only didn't faze me, it felt like a gift from Heaven. I knew I wouldn't get much flak at home. My foster parents were the chilled out type who believed in letting a kid make mistakes. I started excitedly making my plans.

In less than a day, I was completing an application to Neve Yerushalayim, a women's seminary in Jerusalem. I scanned the questions. "Are both of your parents Jewish by birth? What about your grandparents? Were there any conversions to Judaism in your family?" I called my aunt. She knew about my father's side of the family but had some doubt as to whether my maternal grandmother was Jewish.

It took days until I reached my mother by phone and asked her outright. Her knowledge about her own mother, who had died when my mother was twelve, was very hazy. Her parents were second generation Americans and had grown up in the South. There was no recollection of Judaism being practiced at home. However, she did remember going for visits to an aunt on her mother's side and while there, being taken to church with her cousins.

"Doesn't that mean that your mother's family wasn't Jewish?" I asked hoarsely.

She couldn't be sure of anything, she said.

I hung up with a terrible heaviness in my stomach. At this point, I was keeping kosher and was starting to keep Shabbos. Was I Jewish or not? I felt very Jewish, but by now, I already knew that Judaism is not based on feelings, but on clear-cut absolutes: right or wrong, true or false.

I walked around like a zombie for a few days. I tried to pray, but what kind of prayer could I say, "G–d, please make me be a Jew?" I finally called one of the rabbis I knew and just broke down and cried. "If I'm not a Jew, then what am I?" I sobbed. "Was all that suffering I went through in high school for nothing?"

The rabbi calmed me down, saying there was no reason to make any assumptions before doing a complete check into my family tree. There were ways to get at the facts and he would help me, he said. In the meantime, I should conduct myself exactly as before.

He said that the fact that my parents had grown up in the South was encouraging. Jews living there a few generations ago had to contend with widespread anti-Semitism. Fear might have compelled some people to hide their Jewishness or to live as Christians.

Every piece of information I could give him went down on his notepad, and then he gave me my share of the assignment. I was to find out names of cities where my parents had lived, and names and phone numbers of every single relative I could turn up from both sides. For three weeks, I was like a person obsessed, calling relatives who were half-strangers, probing for the missing facts that would spell out my future.

At the time, I was living in a Catholic college dormitory because of the cheap rent. But I had stopped eating out with my friends and hanging out together on Friday nights and Saturday. In fact, I was starting to get flak from friends who felt I was going overboard on this "Jewish thing."

"You're burning your bridges," one friend warned me. "You're going to feel shortchanged."

"I don't think so."

"How can you be sure? I bet you miss the old ways even now."

She was right. There *were* things I did miss.

"Look, why don't you try going back to the way things were for a day. See how you feel. Being Jewish is okay, but make sure you're not going off the deep end."

It was Friday night. I let myself be talked into going to one of the dance clubs I used to go to with the gang. I dressed in my pants and a silk shirt, and we took a cab to the club. "After all," I told myself," it's very likely I'm not even Jewish. I better get used to it."

But my heart was hammering all the way. Music always used to sweep me right in, and I could dance for hours without stopping. But now I couldn't dance; I couldn't eat. I made some excuse and left the club. I started walking. Over an hour later, I was still confused and pondering: "Who am I? Where do I belong? I'm living in a Catholic dormitory while I dream about Neve Yerushalayim, in Israel! I can't go on this way much longer."

The next day, I was supposed to eat the Shabbos morning meal with a family in town. I knew it was wrong of me not to show, but I was feeling too down. I went back to bed and just slept most of the day. The phone call came that night, after Shabbos. It was the rabbi. Just hearing the happiness in his "Gut Voch!" made my heart flip-flop.

"Betty, I have good news for you," he began, but I didn't even hear the rest. I was crying. I kept repeating, "Are you sure? But are you sure?"

Finally, he calmed me down enough to ask me a question that made me realize how deeply he had dug into my lineage. "Why didn't you tell me your great-grandfather on your mother's side was Reuben Elliot Samuelson who married Rachel Schoen, raised five daughters, and in 1884, founded the Hebrew Free Loan Society in Chattanooga, Texas?"

There was nothing I wanted to hear more about than my newfound Jewish relatives, but first I had to make a phone call. I blubbered my thanks and searched in frenzy for Rabbi Moskowitz's number. I hadn't spoken to him in over a month, ever since I began to doubt my Jewishness. I couldn't even bring myself to return his phone calls.

Now I wanted him to know, contrary to what he must have thought, that I hadn't gotten cold feet. If he hadn't given up on me, if his offer was still good, I'd be on that plane to Israel in a heartbeat. I would dance across the threshold of this new life with the joy and gratitude only someone who's been searching long and desperately for her Jewish roots can feel. And I'd celebrate my newfound status in a place I already loved—*Israel!*

Wilner Gohn
and Me

Rhoda's Story

We used to throw around an expression in my family when I was growing up that originated with my grandparents. You know how people joke, "He's not exactly an Einstein," to convey that the person's not too bright? In my grandparents' house, it came out a little differently: "What were you expecting, Wilner Gohn"?

That was my grandparents' metaphor for a genius. All they knew about the legendary Mr. Gohn was that, according to family tradition, he was a world-famous Jewish genius who lived in Poland or Russia a few hundred years ago. He was listed in Grandma's carefully researched family tree, and she took pride in the mystique of extraordinary brilliance that came with the name.

Her parents emigrated from Russia in the early 1900s. They settled in a small town on Long Island, where my great-grandfather eventually made it big buying and selling scrap metal. Even while Grandma was growing up, Judaism already had become an anachronism in their lives. But Grandma had this thing about lineage. Keeping track of the family tree was very important to her.

To tell the truth, that was pretty much all I knew of my Jewish heritage. By the time I reached the age of 40, I felt vaguely aware that something was off balance in my life. I started to explore Judaism, but I was becoming discouraged. Although I'd had a bat mitzvah when I was twelve, I could barely read Hebrew. I was completely unfamiliar with Jewish concepts, practices, and history. Yet, something kept drawing me back to the classes.

My three teenagers thought I'd gone off the deep end. I had been a high school teacher for as long as they could remember, and suddenly, here I was trying to switch gears and become a student. I was wading into foreign waters, acting—in their words—like a teenager, usurping their role.

"Why are you doing this?" my 14-year son old would grumble. "It's weird."

"All this digging into the olden days. Why do you care what some old Jews in Europe did hundreds of years ago?" another complained. "Why do you have to copy all this old-fashioned stuff?"

"Don't tell me we're going kosher!"

My husband, Sid, had been raised in a home that revered twentieth-century norms, believing that ours was an age of enlightenment. How could he understand my frustration that a society that could build rockets and find cures for dreaded diseases could still be in total darkness when it comes to the most fundamental questions: Why are we here? How did we get here? What is the purpose of human suffering?

He knew that these questions bothered me, and he tried to be supportive, but he clearly thought I was just going through a phase. Any day now, he figured, I'd take up scrap-booking or some other pastime instead.

My mother was much more critical. "Why do you need to complicate your life? Get yourself a good therapist if you have a problem!" When I experimented with keeping kosher, I had to turn down invitations that included luncheons and dinners at restaurants. To my mother, that was social suicide. "Your neighbors don't understand you," she'd rail. "You're embarrassing your family."

Then came the revelation about Wilner Gohn. I was in a class on the basics of Judaism offered by the Jewish Heritage Center in Long Island when one of the rabbis quoted someone named "the Vilna Gaon." He explained that this was a seventeenth-century rabbi, regarded as the greatest Torah authority of his generation, as well as a brilliant and prolific author.

My jaw dropped. Could this be my ancestor? I blurted out that

I believed I was a descendant of his, and it was the rabbi's turn to be taken aback. "Are you sure?" he blinked in surprise.

"Well, my grandmother always talked about our great ancestor, Wilner Gohn," I assured him.

"Wilner...?...Oh, Wilner Gohn. I see!" The rabbi was clearly amused but became serious when he saw how eager I was to hear about the legendary rabbi.

The discovery that I was a descendant of a righteous Jewish sage who was also a genius in mathematics and other disciplines was a turning point in my life. It filled me with a sense of vindication. I felt there was an invisible cord connecting me to a valuable legacy that had gotten lost.

Shortly afterward, at the rabbi's urging, I went with my husband to a Gateways seminar. We sat with hundreds of Jews from every kind of background, profession, and social stratum. There were people like myself, people who were close in age to my parents' and a whole contingent of university kids my son's age, sitting at lectures together— not at a Broadway show or at a baseball game, but in classes on Judaism! It felt surreal.

The only Judaism I'd known about till now had nothing to offer twentieth-century people. It was a sentimental leftover from the past, overshadowed by New Age ideas that for me were far more compelling. But as I listened to one lecture after another during the weekend, it seemed that Judaism has morphed into something profound and meaningful. Only gradually did I realize that it wasn't Judaism that had morphed. It was generations of Jews who knew nothing of their heritage that had turned the religion into a bunch of outdated folklore and legends.

A lecture called *Bearers of the Torch: The Unbroken Tradition* opened an entirely new line of thought. The speaker gave a sweep of

Jewish history that put you right in the center of a timeline. You could almost see a panorama of history, from the earliest days of the Jewish nation through a 2,000-year exile until present times. You could examine some of the evidence—the laws like *tefillin* and *tzitis* that are observed exactly the same way today, as the Oral Law instructs.

I learned how Jews from all corners of the globe have identical Torah scrolls, and wear identical *tefillin* and have the same exact *mezuzos*. The rabbi made a compelling point. If the laws were not G–d-given but man-made, wouldn't hundreds, if not thousands, of variations have crept into the style and substance of these objects over the course of 3,000 years? Other speakers elaborated on the same theme that G–d himself, not Moses or any other human being, formulated the Torah, every single word of it, and invested it with immortality.

I had seen *mezuzahs* in a Judaica store, but I never in my life saw the *tefillin* the rabbi mentioned. Later, I overheard one of the lecturers explaining to someone what *tefillin* are—leather straps worn around the arm and the head during prayer, with portions of the Torah written inside small boxes that were attached to the forehead and arm. The idea, he said, was to sanctify ones actions and thoughts to do the will of G–d.

I tried to visualize this, but couldn't imagine any rational, intelligent person tying himself up in leather straps every day in order to pray! How wearisome, I thought, to go through this cumbersome ritual every single day. I much preferred a religion of the spirit to one so laden with rituals and physical obligations.

Hours later, I was in the lobby of the hotel when a crowd began surging excitedly toward the dining room. Sid and I were swept along and soon found out what all the commotion was about. Rabbi Suchard, whose wife had given birth a week before, had arranged to have a circumcision ceremony for the baby. We squeezed ourselves into the hall with everyone else.

Sid pointed to the back of the room, to someone wrapped in

a prayer shawl. When he turned around, I was dumbfounded. It was Rabbi Suchard. Wound around his arm and encircling his head were leather straps, with a black box on his forehead—the *tefillin* I had been trying to visualize just moments before!

I had never before attended a traditional circumcision. A dignified-looking man with a white beard said the prayers and Rabbi Suchard said a blessing. Complete silence. Then the baby cried, more prayers were chanted and hundreds of *Mazel tovs* rang out. People thronged around the radiant parents, hugging and congratulating them. And there I was, tears streaming down my face, as if this joyous occasion were my very own!

Later, as I was trying to understand why this event hit me so deeply, that strange urge to weep reawakened in me. My thoughts kept stealing back to the immense outpouring of joy, an exultation that filled the entire room. What was everyone so happy about? Why the celebration? Babies are born every day.

It had something to do with the concept of the eternity of the Jewish people that was so often evoked during the weekend…Yes, that was it! Right at this circumcision were the key elements of that continuing heritage. The "bearers of the torch"…here they were! Jewish parents making sure that their eight-day-old baby would have the right start in this world. And reminding everyone present that we are all members of an eternal family, that we know the secret of survival.

I later found out that Rabbi Suchard's own father performed the circumcision: one generation passing down a sacred trust to a second, and then to a third. How could you not cry?

I thought about how Jewish tradition had unraveled in my own family and in Sid's so many generations ago, and how hard it would be for us to sew the broken threads together again. Our kids are clearly not interested at this point. They roll their eyes any time I refer to something I've learned in one of my classes.

But when I get discouraged, I think, what can I expect from kids we raised in a society that debunks faith and tradition? If only I knew what I know now when my kids were little—if only I could turn back the clock. Sid keeps reminding me I have to have realistic expectations of myself as well as others.

He's been very accommodating till now, but I wonder where he'll draw the line: No driving on Shabbos, okay; lighting candles, *Kiddush*, Sabbath meal, okay. But no TV, no music, no telephone—not just for one experimental Shabbos, but for *every single Saturday of the year?*

The rabbis advise me to go slow. Don't spend five hours on morning prayers. Don't jump into Shabbos observance all at once. It's never a good idea to make rapid transitions, they say. But I cheat a little, and do more than they suggest. I'm impatient. I want to be a bona fide Jew, and I'm not even half-way home. I want to access that incredible joy again. Maybe it's because I feel the clock ticking. And just maybe it's the pull of my great ancestor, the Vilna Gaon, may his name be blessed.

Not Without
a Fight

Miriam's Story

My father died when I was nine, in the midst of trying to bring our family out of Iran. There was one hitch after another, but after my father's death, as if by magic, a door just seemed to open. Suddenly we had visas, and there was a legal route out of the country. We didn't have to sneak away, terrified of being caught and killed.

All of this help came from my mother's brother, who was already living in America. He wasn't a rich man but he used every penny he had to bring us over. Little by little, a few at a time, he eventually brought out all his relatives. It took about five years. There were over 50 of us, including second cousins. My uncle not only paid for visas and tickets, he found apartments for everyone, so when we arrived in the United States, we weren't homeless.

Although he was relatively young, this uncle became the patriarch of the family. He and his daughter, Esther, had a profound effect on my life. My uncle was religious, and in my mind, his kindness and his religious beliefs were inseparable. Even those in the family who weren't religious deeply respected him.

My cousin, Esther, who was three years older than me, immediately became my inspiration. I looked up to her and tried to follow her example. The first time I spent Shabbat with them, she introduced me to Shabbat observance with complete confidence that I would accept it. "We don't turn on lights on Shabbat," she told me firmly. "We don't travel or shop or drive around. Shabbat is for being close to Hashem."

Her words had such a ring of authority, it didn't occur to me to question her. I was under her spell. She attended a religious school in Brooklyn, and I followed her there. She helped me break the ice that first year, but then she went on to high school. I felt abandoned. Most of my other cousins had taken a different route. They'd gone to public school where they soon blended in with the multi-cultural student body.

By contrast, being Iranian and Sephardic made me feel conspicuous and spurned in the girl's yeshivah I attended. As an orphan, I felt even more inadequate. All through high school, loneliness was my shadow.

Everything changed when another cousin of mine was finally brought over from Iran. Daniel was nineteen, very clever and ambitious. In less than a year, he was further ahead in his education in this country than many Iranians who had come long before him. While studying engineering in college, he even slowly built a small business on the side.

He was dazzling. We became engaged a few months after we met and I was in seventh heaven. And yet...I began to feel torn. Daniel was from a nonreligious family and had very little interest in religion. We were poles apart in our beliefs. We kept trying—and failing—to find a point where we could meet philosophically.

I believed deeply in G–d; Daniel didn't. Our different attitudes toward religion highlighted the great differences in our personalities. My childhood and adolescence had been sad and lonely; from that very loneliness I was drawn to Hashem. Daniel was the exact opposite: charismatic, outgoing, self-assured. He relied on his own intelligence and instincts to determine right and wrong.

Although he said he was willing to keep Shabbat and *kashrut* for me, it didn't take much to foresee that our future would be full of conflict. How would our Shabbat table work? How would I feel knowing my husband doesn't *daven*, doesn't make *berachot*. How could he transmit Judaism to a child?

I tried to connect him with some people who were willing to learn with him. But he was very content with his own lifestyle and had no interest in investigating another path. Soon, I started to drift spiritually. Daniel's opinions, my college environment, and the lack of family support all helped drag me down. My family approved of my "cooling off." They thought I had been way too intense religiously.

As my turmoil grew, I knew I had to talk to someone. I turned to one of my favorite high school teachers, Mrs. Hartman. The first few moments were the hardest. I had been in such a better "place" spiritually when she had last seen me. That was when my dreams of my future centered around marriage to a *ben Torah* and living a Torah life. What would she think of me now?

My words tumbled out haltingly. I tried to explain what had happened to me in the last few years, why I had changed, but I only vaguely understood it. Slowly she drew me out about my relationship with Daniel, the social pressure at school, the loneliness...

After that first talk, we spoke many more times. I knew where she was leading me—but the thought of breaking up with Daniel made me panic. Invitations were about to go out; we had already picked out an apartment and bought furniture.

Yet I couldn't deny it: religious differences had become a major source of contention between us. We had an argument over the family purity laws that left me devastated. Daniel didn't just discourage me; he made it clear that he was vehemently opposed. It was too extreme, he said. He could never get used to it.

I cried so hard that night. I ached in a way that I never knew a heart could hurt. I always believed—and prayed so hard—that he would come around. Now I saw that this was exactly what he assumed about me—that I'd soften up and become more "normal." I knew that no matter how committed we were to each other, we couldn't build a life together on such a shaky foundation.

I knew what I had to do, but felt utterly incapable of doing it. I pictured trying to break up with Daniel and getting into a heavy, emotional scene. He still had a hold over me. I was sure I couldn't withstand his arguments.

But the strangest part was that when it actually happened, there were no fireworks at all. No one shed a tear, no one raised his voice. The breakup had been coming for a while, and I guess we were both prepared for it on some level. We said a bittersweet goodbye, parting as friends.

I wanted to go away immediately afterwards, far away so I wouldn't have to face people. I thought of going to Israel. But my teacher persuaded me to wait a few weeks. She urged me to go to a Gateways retreat at the end of December. I was grieving, and, paradoxically, I needed both privacy and the feeling that I wasn't alone. She said the retreat would offer me that mix.

She turned out to be right about that. It was comforting—and amazing—to be among so many searching people. But there were some very vulnerable moments. One class about the sanctity of the Jewish home hit a raw nerve. Halfway through it, I started crying. But these were not tears of sadness. Suddenly, I knew deep in my heart what a tragic mistake I had come so close to making. I was crying out of relief.

Once before in my life, when I escaped Iran with my family and came to the United States, I had the sense of a door to freedom swinging open. At Gateways, too, I felt that sense of an "opening," of an exhilarating trip that didn't end when it was officially over. The inspiration, the connections with new friends, the new link with Hashem…all this kept me going, long after I came home.

A couple of weeks afterward, I was on my way to a Torah retreat in New Jersey, and made plans to catch a ride with people leaving from Monsey on a Friday afternoon. Never having been to Monsey, I miscalculated the distance from Brighton Beach, took a very late bus and arrived in Monsey so late, I missed my ride.

I was stranded in a town where I knew no one.

I considered my options: take a bus home (not enough time before Shabbat); take a taxi to the seminar (I wasn't sure of the location); or beg for help from the first passerby.

It was bitterly cold and no one was around. I stood on the street with the icy wind battering me, Shabbat a mere hour away. Panic rose in my chest. Where on earth in this strange town could I go? Tears of despair flowed down my cheeks. Then, out of nowhere, a young Chasidic-looking man called over to me, "Are you in some kind of trouble?" I nodded and blurted out that I'd missed my ride and didn't know anyone in this town. He had a car nearby and offered to drive me to his mother-in-law's home a few blocks away, where I could make arrangements for Shabbat.

At the mother-in-law's home, I continued trying to make connections to get to the weekend retreat. But it was useless. The mother-in-law looked at me biting back tears of disappointment and said gently, "*Mamale*, don't be upset. It must be *bashert* that you should be here for Shabbos. Everything's going to be all right."

I managed a weak smile and dialed Mrs. Hartman's number, choking up as I described how I'd missed my ride and was completely lost. "Don't worry," she reassured me, "A Jew can't get lost in Monsey. Let me make a phone call to someone I know and get right back to you."

She called back in a few minutes with astonishing news: a women's seminar was taking place in Monsey that very Shabbat at Ohr Somayach, and accommodations could easily be arranged for me to attend!

To make a long story short, I ended up eating the Shabbat morning *seudah* in the home of one of the seminar hosts, Rabbi and Rebbetzin Swiatycki. As I was thanking them for their hospitality, Mrs. Swiatycki took me aside and told me she had a wonderful idea for a *shidduch* for me! I was so shocked I didn't know what to say.

She went on to describe the boy as a refined *ben Torah* who had been a *talmid* in the Ohr Somayach Yeshiva, and still kept in close touch with his *rebbeim*. His background was Iranian, like mine. I tried to explain that I had just finalized plans to go to Israel to study at a women's seminary, that I wasn't in any frame of mind to start dating. But the *rebbetzin* was so persuasive; she talked me into agreeing to just one meeting.

"You never know from where your *bashert* will come," she said. Why not give it just one chance?"

As fantastic as it sounds, that is how I met my husband! Now, six months later, I'm still in awe of the amazing way the pieces to this puzzle all came together. I think of all the pain I had to go through until I was ready to meet Aharon … the broken engagement, the despair and loneliness… I think back to how hard I fought to get out of Monsey that *erev Shabbat* when I was "supposed" to be going somewhere else. And how frantic I was to leave that town—the very place where my *bashert* was waiting for me!

I just hope I never forget how Hashem literally had to force me to that spot—fighting and crying all the way—in order to receive His blessing.

Promises
to Keep

*Sylvia Roth had never married, and after the death of her mother,
lived by herself. At 71, she had outlived her few immediate relatives,
and was literally alone in the world. She knew little about Judaism
beyond its cultural and culinary aspects. Her late-blooming hunger to
learn more about her heritage had been sparked by her friendship with
a warmhearted religious family who had "adopted" her.*

Sylvia's Story

My neighbors, Chana and her husband, Zev, are from Russia.
Their children have never met their grandparents on either side. They
need a Bubby and I need a few precious grandchildren, so we kind of
adopted each other.

You know, I have my own little clique of friends in my
neighborhood. We play bridge, go to a show, and even take trips together.
But Chana and Zev are in a different category. They're like the daughter
and son I never had. They invite me over every single Shabbos and for
every holiday. They share their lives with me, and my whole life has
changed because of them.

I was raised without any Jewish education, because my mother
herself had none. Oh, she knew about fasting on Yom Kippur, and for
some strange reason, she never sewed on Shabbos. But she didn't keep
the other restrictions. We also kept two sets of dishes, but we weren't
that careful about keeping kosher.

Yet all my life I heard about a promise my father made to his
mother on her deathbed. He was only 23 when she died, and he vowed
to remain religious. It was a promise kept more in spirit than in deed
because, in my parents' world, you were a good Jew if you were honest
and kind, believed in G–d, and never hurt anyone.

That was my philosophy, too, until Zev tried to educate me. He
said, "Sylvia, that's the definition of a good Gentile. Being a good Jew

means much, much more." I was very offended when he told me that! All my life I've been proud of being Jewish. I didn't want to hear that my family's observance of Judaism was inferior.

My friends rallied behind me. "Orthodox Jews are holier-than-thou and intolerant," they said. But I knew this didn't describe Zev and Chana, because they are the most loving and giving people you'll ever meet. So I couldn't stay angry because I really love them. They're all the family I have.

Remember a few years ago, when we had the winter of twelve snowstorms? Chana gave birth right during a blizzard. Afterward, her friends wanted to bring her food and she begged them not to, because the roads were so icy. Well, she was wasting her breath. You have no idea what those people did for her, how much food they brought, some on foot, some by car. The kindness in the religious community is simply astounding.

When I came into a large inheritance after my uncle's death, I felt a strong need to do something with it that would make a difference. I looked into many Jewish charities and I almost signed a contract with a Jewish foundation. But then Zev told me about the holiness of a Torah scroll and how it's been the cornerstone of Judaism for over 3,000 thousand years. And he told me about a Rabbi Steinman whom he got to know when he was studying in Israel, before he met Chana. He told me what a righteous and humble person he is, and how his yeshivah doesn't own its own Torah scroll. Well, I thought to myself, maybe I can do something about that.

Not long ago, I went to a Gateways seminar (thanks to Chana's prodding!) and I met up with a very nice woman named Naomi, who helped out at the seminar. We ended up going to some classes together and sitting together at mealtimes. I found myself telling her about my wonderful trip to Israel a few months ago. I described the highlight, my first-ever *Hachnosas Sefer Torah*. It was sensational. Thousands of people streamed into Bnei Brak, from as far away as Hebron, to celebrate together.

All I had to do was close my eyes and it all came rushing back. …The music… flaming torches lighting up the night… little children marching… people dancing on rooftops, packed together on balconies watching the parade…

"If I didn't have pictures, I would have thought I dreamed all this!" I told Naomi.

"You didn't by chance bring any with you?" she asked hopefully.

"No, unfortunately not… But I'll try to describe it. And let me tell you how I happened to be connected to this wonderful event."

I described the scene of thousands of people standing up and singing as Rabbi Steinman came in to the hall and the tremendous happiness I felt that I was a part of it. "I have to tell you, when I saw that Torah scroll in his arms – and the silver crown I bought for it – I felt so elated. You've never seen anything so magnificent! But the most wonderful thing of all was this rabbi's blessing to me—"

"To *you?*" Naomi's eyes widened.

"Yes, to me. That was after the whole thing was over. He blessed me that the Torah I gave him should bring sanctity into my life and be a source of merit for me."

Naomi's jaw dropped. "…the Torah you *gave* him?"

"Yes, my dear, that's what I'm about to tell you. His yeshivah had three others, but they were all borrowed. The one I just gave him belongs to him and the yeshivah."

"You mean, it was *yours?* Where in the world did you get it?"

"I commissioned it from a Rabbi Helprin in Israel, who writes Torah scrolls for a living. Chana's husband, Zev, actually studied with this Rabbi Helprin. That's how the whole idea of donating the Torah scroll came about."

"Amazing. Writing a sefer Torah for Rav Steinman just like that.... ! What made you decide to do that?"

"Well, my mother died a few years ago. She would have been 99 on her next birthday. She was a wonderful human being. I gave this Torah in honor of her third *yahrzeit*, in memory of my parents."

Naomi seemed strangely moved. She asked me more about my parents and about my life. She was fascinated by the sefer Torah episode. She said, "I bet if you were able to trace your parents' lineage back a few centuries, you'd find a connection somewhere to Rav Steinman's ancestors. There's absolutely nothing random in this world, although we rarely get to see the whole picture." *What an amazing idea*, I thought.

We ended up talking for over an hour. Our conversation turned to why I'd come to the weekend retreat. I told her that as much as I respect Chana and Zev, as beautiful as their lifestyle is, it didn't prove to me that their way is the only way to live. So, that's what brought me to Gateways.

"It wasn't an easy decision coming here," I explained. "Look around; the average age is about 35-40. I'm on the ancient side. But my mind is still sharp. One of the rabbis said, 'Weigh the evidence and judge for yourself.' And that's what I'm doing."

It's already a few weeks since I came home and I've been doing a lot of thinking. The classes answered a lot of questions for me, but also created new ones. It seems to me it all comes down to one thing: the claim that G–d really spoke to the Jewish people, gave them the Torah, and said it must be followed for the rest of time. If that's true, where does that leave me?

In a way, I'm like my father, who had no peace. He had given his word to his dying mother, but I think he had doubts about how well he was carrying it out—*if* he was carrying it out. Maybe that commitment he made transferred to me, somehow. I've started to light candles Friday night and I say the blessing that Chana taught me. Sometimes I cry when I do it. At my age, I get emotional easily.

I learned a lot about the Jewish soul at the seminar. One of the speakers said that *Olam haba* means the world that *comes from this one*. It's what you do in this world that creates a place for your soul in the next one. I've been kind of dwelling on that thought.

Every time I tell myself, "Sylvia, you're too old to change your lifestyle," I think of my parents. I imagine my father saying, "Silky," (that's what he called me) "if you can pull this off, it'll be a comfort to me and Mama here." And maybe my mother is smiling and saying, "Yes, it'll be a gift to us—as magnificent as the Torah you gave in our memory."

I get all teary-eyed when I let my mind wander this way. But it's more than just a sweet little daydream. There's a feeling of real urgency to all this because I'm their only descendant and no one lives forever. If I don't keep my father's pledge, who will?"

Etched
In Stone

Vivian's Story

Before my husband and I were married, when our relationship was first turning serious, we happened to be out driving one Saturday morning and passed a synagogue. It was about 11:30 and people were just leaving. Many of the men were wrapped up in long white shawls with fringes sweeping the ground. The men all wore black hats.

I was embarrassed for them, and looked around to see if they were drawing attention to themselves. I mumbled something to Al about Orthodox Jews always needing to overdo it. His rejoinder threw me off balance.

"Is that how you react when you see someone in a turban or a Muslim *hijab?*"

I had to admit it wasn't. He then told me something that blew me away. In his late teens, he said, he had gone on a summer tour of Israel and had ended up on a religious kibbutz. That experience influenced him to start leading a religious lifestyle. When he came back home, he kept it up for a while until, eventually, his motivation fizzled out. Although no longer observant, Al remembered that men wore a *tallis* home from synagogue not to flaunt their religion, but because for religious Jews, carrying on the Sabbath is forbidden.

I felt ashamed for being so judgmental. But I was more disconcerted to hear that Al had once been religious—as if he had once had some kind of disease.

"Would you ever go back to that way of life?" I wanted to know. (Is it possible the disease might recur?)

"No chance."

He sounded pretty definite but an alarm had gone off in my head and was still ringing. "Religious" in my mind meant living a life of stifling restriction and religious authoritarianism.

"Okay, because I could never live that way. It goes totally against my grain. I could never, *ever* marry someone who believed in all that," I said ardently.

He seemed surprised at my vehemence. "Want it etched in stone?" he laughed.

Right then and there, we actually made a pact—part joke, part dead serious—that if we ever decided to get married, we would absolutely never be religious.

It's sixteen years later, and Al and I live in Freehold, New Jersey, with our two children. Our twelve-year-old daughter, Laura, recently prevailed upon us to change her school so she could be with some Jewish friends she made in summer camp. Her new school is Shalom Academy, a religious day school. Al and I decided to make the switch despite our forebodings that the school would try to "proselytize" us into becoming religious.

We made the decision because we were troubled by some unhealthy situations in the public school Laura attended. We heard rumors about a teacher acting inappropriately with some of the kids. Ironically, it took a twelve-year-old's urgings to prod us out of our inertia! Despite our concern, we were acting as though we were basically helpless to change the situation. Laura had to lead the way. It was humbling.

A few months into the school year, we received a flyer from Shalom Academy urging all parents to attend a weekend retreat together with their children, sponsored by the school. Al and I signed up immediately, curious to meet the other parents and to see Laura's new peer group first-hand.

This was our introduction to Gateways, a family-oriented organization that has had a strong impact on us. It's hard to point to one specific class or encounter responsible for that impact; it's the entire… mosaic. A few of the classes, like the ones on anger control and parenting, really spoke to me. There were back-to-back lectures on faith, history, ethics, Shabbos…. a whole gamut of topics.

Over the weekend, I began to realize that the Torah has a unique perspective on human psychology and the ability of people to bring about change in themselves. There's a strong emphasis on self-improvement, but not in the same spirit as Dale Carnegie, where the goal is to learn "how to win friends and influence people." In Judaism, the goal seems to be to draw closer to G–d by bringing tranquility into your life and your relationships with others.

In other words, if you have a sarcastic streak or you're the type to nurse a grudge, it doesn't have to own you. You can and should change, because that's why you're here.

The psychology was great, but Al and I had trouble with some of the more fundamental concepts. Was the Torah literally G–d's word, handed down to the Jewish people over 3,000 years ago through Divine revelation? Was it meant to apply eternally? These seemed fantastic assumptions, difficult to swallow.

Many of the lectures offered strong proof of a Divine Revelation at Sinai. The rabbis had a very broad grasp of Biblical writings and Jewish history and took several approaches to prove that human authorship of the Torah was not just unlikely, but impossible.

For Al and me, an especially moving concept was the image of generations of Jewish parents passing down a legacy to their children century after century, in spite of mass persecution and expulsions. In all corners of the globe, there were Jews who had stubbornly held that torch high. So if Judaism was still on the map today, one had to admit it was only because of those "torch-bearing" Jews.

That generational thing tugged at my heart. I remember my

grandfather as a torch-bearing Jew. I still recall the image of him from my childhood... praying in a *tallis* and *tefillin*. But when he died, his torch lay in the dust. There was no one to pick it up. As far as I was concerned, every vestige of religious Judaism had died along with Grandpa.

That thought had never saddened me when I was younger. Now it did.

Our son, Jay, had his bar mitzvah in our Conservative synagogue. Not surprisingly, once the big day was behind him, Jay showed no interest whatsoever in attending services, or in any other aspect of Judaism for that matter. Even the few Jewish things we did as a family, like some of the festive aspects of the holidays, held little appeal for him.

Once, that thought might not have saddened me particularly. Now it did.

In the days after that first Gateways seminar, we pondered the thought that without Jewish pride and Jewish identity, without practicing authentic Judaism, or seeing it practiced, our children had not more than a 50% chance of marrying someone Jewish. And those odds would narrow drastically for our grandchildren, if by some miracle they were born Jewish. In our own lifetimes, we realized with sinking hearts, we might witness the total cut-off of our family's Jewish line.

The pact Al and I had made, that promise etched in stone that we would never, ever become religious, suddenly started to disintegrate. It seemed childish and irrelevant now.

Over the course of the next four months, during which we attended three more Gateways events, Al and I came to a decision. We could not afford the luxury of exploring Judaism in the slow and leisurely way we would have preferred. That slow journey—a few classes here and there, a seminar once in a while, until we had the 100% clarity that would justify a complete lifestyle change—was for people with very young children.

For us, with one teenager and one pre-teen, time was of the essence. People we met at various seminars, who were making the journey back to their Jewish roots in mid-life, confided how terribly hard it was on the family, how much tension and alienation it caused when older children, quite naturally, resisted the changeover to a religious lifestyle.

That realization galvanized us. We threw ourselves into frenzied learning. The Gateways staff was a tremendous help. After launching us on the journey, they made certain we had a broad array of "rest stops" along the way. Working together with local outreach groups, they guided us from one milestone to another.

For a while, I was taking three morning classes and two evening classes a week. Al came home from work, ate supper quickly, and was off to his evening classes several times a week.

Four months after our first seminar, we had koshered our home, were keeping the laws of family purity, and steadily increasing our Sabbath observance. If we hadn't believed in Divine Providence before then, something incredible happened that left no doubt that Hashem was orchestrating things.

We were thrilled that Laura was doing beautifully in her day school, but felt stymied when it came to finding an approach that would persuade our son to switch from public school to yeshivah. What would possibly motivate this young man to leave his pleasant and familiar high school environment where he was at the top of his class, came home at 2:30, and had plenty of free time? In a yeshivah, he'd be a total stranger, know less than the class dummy, and have to be in school until 5:00 or 6:00 pm. We felt licked before we began.

But that locked door suddenly swung wide open. Before we even broached the subject of transferring to yeshivah, Jay began having some trouble in school. He came home complaining of a few class bullies picking on him, being physically and verbally abused, even once locked inside a closet. Al and I looked at each other in disbelief.

Seizing on this development, we began talking to Jay about the advantages of a private school. Eventually—in order to escape the harassment at school—he agreed to try out a yeshivah. We found one with a good introductory program, where a car pool had already been set up for commuters.

Starting at the bottom hasn't been easy for Jay. The whole transition to a religious life has been a difficult struggle for him.

I used to believe that the most important task of parenthood is to raise ethical and kind children. Now I know there is no morality or ethics without G–d. Recently, a sensational case of mercy-killing was in the news. Advocates say euthanasia is the highest form of mercy. On the opposite side of the fence, it's considered flat-out murder. Which is it? Without putting G–d in the picture—right in the center—how can anyone be sure they're not doing something criminal, disguised as something noble?

And I used to think that being religious stifled human nature. When I sat *shivah* for my mother a few weeks ago, I discovered how misguided I was. I thought I knew all about *shivah*, from having lost my father three years earlier, when we still belonged to the Conservative synagogue.

Shivah was a grand, week-long party, where people piled in and your role was to provide the food and entertainment. Laughter, jokes and bantering dominated the scene. You wouldn't even know anyone died! Then the party is abruptly over, and you're alone. People expect you to stop crying and get up and go back to business. Except you can't. You haven't even begun to grieve.

When my mother died, after we became religious, I cringed at the thought of going through *shivah* again. But then I found out how this practice is actually supposed to be observed. Families in Lakewood with whom Al and I had become friendly came with an outpouring of practical help and emotional support. They explained that the laws of mourning ease the mourner's grief, but are primarily for the benefit of the soul of the departed. The idea that true solace comes from giving the dead their proper due at the time of death was completely novel to me.

Our Lakewood friends thought of every conceivable thing I would need to observe *shivah* properly. They offered their comfort quietly. There was no trace of the partying and gaiety I so dreaded. Those who came to visit drew me out about my mother. As painful as it was, I found I needed to talk about her, not try to hide my grief.

One of the women offered to learn the laws of mourning with me. Questions about the afterlife arose as we went though the laws. I clung to the assurance that my mother's soul was alive in the World of Truth, and that through my own deeds and those of my children, I could bring elevation to her soul.

My thoughts kept streaming back to how she had been so bewildered by our becoming religious; she had been disappointed in me and had slowly withdrawn emotionally. It gave me comfort to know that now, in the World of Truth, she at last understood. I pictured her smiling reassuringly, no longer hurt and distant. I pictured her healthy, vibrant... and above all, having *nachas*.

Jew
Without
a Name

Jennifer's Story

When I was about eleven, a boy in my school called a Jewish kid a terrible name. The Jewish kid shot back, "Call me any name you want, just make sure you put the word 'Jew' in there!"

My friend, Gloria, turned to me, "You hear that? He's even proud of it!"

"Why shouldn't he be?" I said.

Gloria gave me a funny look. "I forgot. You're Jewish yourself, because of your mother."

"No I'm not!" I exclaimed indignantly. "I'm not Jewish any more than you are."

She shrugged, unconvinced. I checked this situation out with my mother. "Gloria says I'm Jewish. 'If your mother's Jewish then *you* are,' that's what she said," I told my mother, afraid that it might be true.

"You were baptized as a baby. Baptizing makes you a full-fledged Christian," she reassured me.

"You mean I'm not even *half-Jewish*?" Boy, wouldn't Gloria be surprised. But a thought occurred to me. "How come you were never baptized yourself?" I asked.

"Because I never converted," she said. "Anyway, it wouldn't have made a difference."

I was dumbfounded. Why not, I wondered. Why wouldn't it make a difference? But Mom switched the subject in a way that made it clear that further questions were off limits. Left to my own conclusions, I decided that once you were a certain age, baptism was no longer effective in getting rid of Jewishness.

Only much later, when I was in college, did I realize the truth: My mother never had herself baptized because she knew the whole thing was a bunch of nonsense! That revelation made me angry. There were certain things she had obviously felt compelled to do with us children as a concession to my father, who was Catholic. But to tell your Jewish children that they were *full-fledged Christians*! Denying them even that "half-Jew" status that might have kept alive a spark of identity, a spark of loyalty to the faith of their ancestors? It was incomprehensible that she had chosen to keep me totally in the dark.

Glancing back at my mother's family history, it should not have been so mystifying. My grandparents were Rumanian. They had immigrated to America before the war and were completely nonobservant. Three of their four children married Christians. And the next generation intermarried entirely. Nobody seemed to care.

The only self-identifying Jew in the whole clan was Aunt Elaine. She and Uncle Henry would host a huge Passover dinner each year at which there were more non-Jews in our multi-cultural family than Jews. Everyone came because it was a thoroughly enjoyable social event. Traditional touches such as the food—"kosher-style" matzah balls, gefilte fish with horseradish, brisket, kugel and borscht—were combined with contemporary New Age cuisine.

Although I had been raised Catholic, by the time I was fifteen, I no longer attended church or observed any religious rituals. It all seemed empty and meaningless to me.

The first religious Jew I ever met was a Chasidic computer technician named Hank (no one could pronounce his Jewish name), who worked at the firm where I was first employed. Besides being the only Jew in the place (unless you counted "half-Jews" like me), he was the only one who really understood the systems we were using and could solve the innumerable computer jams perplexing our employees.

The weird thing about him was that he was totally non-ambitious and quite happy that way. Despite being a genius at what he did, he didn't seem to want to get ahead. He said he preferred studying in his yeshivah, and only came to the office once or twice a week, or for an emergency. For a while, computer emergencies at the firm were the norm, so on any given day, he had a backlog of a dozen people frantically trying to reach him. Most of them couldn't get through.

He always returned my calls, though. I once asked him why I could reach him when others couldn't, and he said because it's a *mitzvah*—a G–d given commandment—to help a fellow Jew. I was secretly pleased but pretended to be indignant. "You mean helping a non-Jew is not considered a good deed?" I asked.

"It is, but it's not on the same level as helping a Jew," he said.

I finally asked him what I'd been itching to know for a long time. "Why do you believe in G–d?" I blurted out.

He was silent for a moment. Then he said, "Look, if I told you and you really understood, it would change your life, and you're probably not ready for that."

That stopped me. It wasn't that my life was so great I couldn't imagine changing it. But I'm not the daring type who can swim upstream while everyone's going the other way. So I didn't press the issue. But what evolved from that short conversation is that after confirming that my mother was Jewish, Hank suggested I spend a Shabbos at the home of a religious family he knew in Brooklyn. He offered to set up the arrangements if I were interested. I was. That was my introduction to the world of religious Jews, a world I never could have conceived of in my deepest imagination.

The visit with Hank's friends, the Bergers, a Chasidic family of twelve, was more than a culture shock. It shook up many misconceptions I had heard and accepted about religious Jews, and Chasidim in particular. I found out religious people are not the rigid, unapproachable people who look right through you when you pass them on the street. True, they've got that forbidding mystique and you can't help but expect an icy reception as you muster your nerve and actually enter their domain—but once you cross their doorstep, it's a completely different story.

The warmth and kindness I was treated with overwhelmed me. The little children seemed in awe of me. They competed with each other to teach me what I needed to know to keep Shabbos. One of them, a little six-year-old girl, was baffled at my ignorance. "How come you don't know anything?" she asked, feeling sorry for me.

"I wasn't lucky enough to go to the kind of school you go to."

"Why didn't your mother teach you?"

"She doesn't know about it either."

"Well, what about your father?"

"He's not even Jewish."

Her eyes grew as round as saucers. She was aghast. *"How could your mother do that? Marry a goy!"*

That was my first inkling that intermarriage is an unthinkable tragedy to this community.

The Bergers were my stepping stone to a whole network of families that only needed to hear one line, "Hello—I'm your Shabbos guest," before melting into a pulsing orbit of friendliness and hospitality. I found it easy to keep Shabbos in their homes—at least publicly. But privately, I did what I wanted, using hot water in the bathroom, for example, or checking my e-mail on my laptop computer in the privacy of my room. I never got into philosophical discussions with the families I visited, always keeping in mind Hank's daunting words: "Forget it. If I told you and you really understood, it would change your life…"

It wasn't until my first Gateways seminar that the philosophical underpinnings of Judaism hit me full force. I had come at the recommendation of a religious friend who promised that one three-day seminar would be equivalent in inspiration and learning to a whole year of Shabbos visits with religious families.

I was conflicted. I was hungry to know more, but I was afraid of the consequences: I might have to make sweeping changes in my life.

That first seminar was exactly three years ago. What I remember most about it was the wonderful feeling that I was no longer an outsider in a religious environment. I would never have defined myself as religious—in fact, I made a point of telling people flat out that I was an atheist. Yet in a strange way, I felt I belonged.

It was comforting that there was a grand scheme to Judaism, not that I understood what it was, nor could I defend it on philosophical (or any other) grounds. But it made me feel secure that Judaism was real, that it was more than Aunt Elaine's once-a-year multi-cultural extravaganza.

Following that seminar, I kept in touch with Gateways through their follow-up programs. I began to learn to read Hebrew, the most non-threatening—and for me, a language-major—the easiest subject in Judaism. But a funny thing happened. Once I could read Hebrew, I began to be interested in the prayers.

Not that I wanted to pray. But I was intrigued by them. At one of the later Gateways seminars I attended, one of the rabbis was explaining the morning prayers and he spent time on the *Asher Yatzar* blessing.

A woman objected that it struck her as unnatural and inappropriate to dwell on bodily functions as part of a prayer. The rabbi answered her that all a person had to do was visit a dialysis ward in a hospital to appreciate the miracle of how our bodies work, and to inspire gratitude to G–d for being healthy. No longer would it seem inappropriate, he said, to thank G–d repeatedly for the blessings of a healthy digestive and excretory system.

That clicked powerfully with me. I knew someone on dialysis and I knew how fervently that person yearned for the gift of a normal life, with normal-functioning kidneys. Gratitude to G–d for one's blessings as the basis for daily prayer suddenly seemed so logical, so… right.

At one seminar, one of the lecturers urged people who had never prayed and didn't know how, to say one small prayer in any language, whether or not it was backed by belief.

"Just start a connection," she said.

My first prayer was no small prayer. I asked G–d for something so big I knew it wouldn't be granted, as if to prove that prayer would never work for me. I asked G–d to cause something to happen to break up my relationship with a non-Jewish friend who I knew was not good for me. On my own, I was helpless to end it.

I said, "Please, G–d, make this person just walk out of my life and not look back."

Believe it or not, barely two weeks later, that is what happened. I thought I would be devastated by getting jilted, but I felt strangely detached. As though my heart was somehow anesthetized.

I tried it again. I asked for clarity about where I stood in Judaism, whether to look at Jewish commitment as a criterion in a prospective husband. Someone had told me that one of the most potent moments of Divine favor takes place at a Jewish wedding, while the *kallah* stands under the *chupah*. That's when I prayed for clarity.

A few days later, the guy I was dating got into a discussion with me about Judaism. He was trying to debunk its Divine origin. He said,

"Do you really think when Adam wrote the Bible…"

"You mean Moses," I cut him off, stifling a laugh. I forgot that I too was once that ignorant.

"Adam, Moses…whatever," he said.

But that was enough. I had my moment of clarity. I knew I couldn't marry someone who was so ignorant about his Jewish heritage.

Here's the irony: Two and a half years after my first Gateways seminar, I was keeping Shabbos and Jewish holidays. I was dressing modestly. I was learning about Jewish customs and laws with a telephone *chavrusah*, but I was still not keeping kosher outside my home. I had more trouble with *kashrus* than anything else.

That summer I found myself at a Torah retreat in Moodus, Connecticut, where one of the teachers, Jill Kaizman, took me in hand. "Jennifer," she said, "do you think your difficulty with *kashrus* is tied in with reluctance to affirming your Jewish identity in public situations? For some reason you can't say, 'I'm an observant Jew; I don't eat in this or that restaurant?'"

As soon as she posed the question, I knew she was right. There were Hank's words, again, ringing in my ears. *You'd have to change your life…* I could keep Shabbos in the privacy of my own house, away from public scrutiny. But keeping kosher meant never eating out with friends, never eating or drinking with them in their homes. Keeping *kashrus* meant severing social ties. I couldn't cross that threshold.

Mrs. Kaizman took a hard line with me. "Just do it. Do it because that's what G–d wants and you don't have a choice in the matter." She cared enough to go even further. One morning, after the men finished *davening*, she arranged for me a kind of informal "naming ceremony" where I was given a Hebrew name for the first time in my life. It was a name I myself had chosen after a lot of thought, and with a heartfelt prayer that it would bring me closer to the Torah.

They called me Yehudit. Since that very emotional moment, Hashem has opened the door not only to *kashrus,* but to many other *mitzvos* and opportunities that have completely changed—*are you ready for this, Hank—I mean Henoch, wherever you are*—that have completely changed my life.

Stained
Glass

Leona's Story

When I was seven years old, my mother refused to let me go with my Catholic neighbor to her church. I kicked up a huge fuss and when that didn't help, I picked myself up and ran away. I had cousins nearby, but knew better than to try to take refuge there. I ran to the nearest neutral territory I could think of—the synagogue.

To this day, I don't know what made me head in that direction. I had been there only once before, on the High Holidays with my parents. The building had an old, musty smell. The rabbi spotted me sulking in the corner and came over to me. He asked me what I was doing there and I told him I had run away from home and that I wanted to change from being Jewish to Catholic. Peering shyly up at his face, I saw that he was taking me very seriously. Behind his thick glasses, he looked worried and sad. "Why would you want to do that?" he asked me gently.

"Because when I get married I want to dress up like the beautiful bride I saw coming out of the church," I told him. I had never seen a bride before and assumed that I had to be Catholic to become one.

"We have beautiful things, too," the rabbi told me.

"Like what?" I asked, a bit astonished.

"Come with me," he said.

He took me inside the small sanctuary and went over to the Holy Ark. It was draped by a blue velvet curtain fringed in gold, with silver and gold embroidered letters decorating it. He moved the curtain, then opened the door behind it and stepped aside to let me see. Two Torah scrolls lay inside, adorned with beautiful, jewel-studded covers. Glistening silver crowns and other wondrous ornaments glinted in the late afternoon sunlight.

"What are they?" I whispered in awe.

"These are Torah scrolls," he told me, letting me feast my eyes before he closed the door. "G–d gave the Torah to the Jewish people to teach them the right way to live. That means the Torah belongs to you and your family, too."

"They're ours —my family's?"

The rabbi smiled down at me, his eyes crinkling at the sides. "Yes, they are partly yours. But they must stay in this cabinet – it's called an *aron kodesh*—where Jews can honor them properly. If you come to *shul* on Shabbos you can see the Torah when it is taken out and read."

On Shabbos, I stood in the empty women's section peeking through the curtain. I gazed at the beautiful stained glass windows and stared at the men with their prayer shawls over their heads, swaying back and forth. With that strange nodding motion of the whole body accompanying the hum of their murmured prayers, it looked as if they were giving their assent to something of great importance. "*Yes, this is the way it is… This is the way it must be.*"

I watched as the rabbi removed the Torah, my Torah, from the Ark. As the men clustered around to kiss it, tears sprang to my eyes. Somewhere in my little girl's mental world, an image had taken root. Jews were kind and gentle people who loved a beautiful scroll that the rabbi said contained teachings from G–d. The rabbi himself seemed larger than life to me.

Many years later, when the influence of my college years left me groping for a spiritual anchor, these childhood memories kept me from drifting far away from the little Judaism I had in my life. They were warm memories of the *shul* and its rabbi who had captured a child's heart by showing her the beautiful treasure in the Holy Ark and making her part "owner" of it.

When my first baby was born, I was so awed by the miracle of his birth that I wanted to say a prayer of thanks. But I had never prayed before. "We have a religion, and a heritage that I know nothing about," I told my husband sadly. "But it's going to be different for our child."

I didn't know how to go about it. For years, I experimented with different approaches and different levels of observance. As my family grew, I kept trying to sweep them along with me as I worked on keeping kosher and having a traditional Shabbos.

When I was growing up, my mother had insisted on having a kosher kitchen (though what we ate outside didn't matter) in deference to her mother. On an impulse, I called her up one day and said, "Ma, I want to make my house kosher. What do I have to do?"

Mom was not impressed. "What's this, your latest *meshugas*? It's expensive and you will have to throw out a lot of things in your kitchen. Are you sure you want to do this?"

"I'm sure," I told her. She came over with some huge pots and a big stone. She filled the pots with water and brought them to a boil. In went my stainless steel pots and pans, as many as could fit. She dropped the stone inside the pot and boiling water overflowed on all sides. Silverware and other kitchen utensils followed. Items that were made partly from plastic or wood we threw away.

Then she went to work on my stove with a blowtorch. After several hours of this, I sank exhausted into a chair, feeling enormously proud of myself. I had a kosher kitchen! What an accomplishment! "Ma, you did it, I'm kosher," I exulted. But her response threw a damper on my joy.

"Listen to me," she said. "The first thing you do now is you go out and buy some paper plates and plastic cutlery. Then, when you can't control your urge to eat *treif*, you take out paper and plastic and eat whatever it is and throw everything away. That way you keep your house kosher!"

"You're telling me to eat *treif?*" I asked her in disbelief.

"G—d forbid. But you can't become kosher overnight. And when you give in to temptation in the beginning, at least it shouldn't *treif* up the whole kitchen."

Compromises and halfway measures were not my mother's nature. She had grown up in a traditional home with European grandparents who slowly watered down their religious observance as they Americanized. Aware of her long-term commitment to *kashrus* all the years of my childhood, I wondered if she longed for the full scope of the religious lifestyle she had seen as a young girl, but had abandoned when she married my father. I never had the courage to ask her.

I plunged ahead with my return to tradition, targeting Shabbos as my next challenge. While my family had grudgingly gone along with becoming kosher, I met stiff resistance on the issue of Shabbos. My husband and kids felt as if they were being railroaded into religion against their will. It took me a long time to understand that Judaism is not simply a collection of rituals and traditions that you can arbitrarily import into your home. The mistakes I made trying to do just that ended up creating friction, alienating my oldest child from Judaism when he was in his teens.

One of the turning points in my life came when Torah Links took root in nearby Cherry Hill, New Jersey. My first contact with this group was a crash course in Hebrew reading. Thanks to Rabbi Mordechai Rhein, I learned how to read Hebrew and to pray from the *siddur*.

The class became a stepping-stone to a deeper involvement in Jewish studies. Shabbatons organized by Torah Links created bonds of friendship, a network of support, and a number of families "testing the waters" of religious observance.

Through Torah Links, we made arrangements to attend a Gateways seminar. With some misgivings, we brought along our two daughters, Elizabeth, 18, and Susan, 14. "Dragged them along" would be more accurate, since they were quite vocally *not* interested in attending. Having two angry, protesting teenagers on my hands for the first half of the seminar nearly ruined the entire experience. Once again, I had allowed my enthusiasm to override my common sense. When would I learn?

But somewhere between Shabbos afternoon and Sunday, my daughters stopped boycotting the classes. They attended a few and grudgingly admitted to enjoying them. And to my utter amazement, Elizabeth thanked me for bringing her.

Liz is a girl who won't take anything "on faith." Before she'll sign on to anything, it's got to stand up to scrutiny, to logic, to science. It's got to be consistent. And it has to sound the right chord to someone with a twenty-first century, very liberal mindset.

She fired her questions at the rabbis without mercy. From my vantage point, I could see the outlines of the huge chip on her shoulder. But they didn't seem to mind. I could see that their scope of knowledge impressed her. By the end of the seminar, she had spoken to one of them about helping her find the right school in Israel for a year of study before starting college. Rabbi Mordechai Becher helped her narrow down the choice of seminaries to the one most suited to her.

Her first letters were full of indignation. She found the seminary – which was considered more liberal than most—"narrow-minded and dogmatic." She challenged every single thing they told her. I suggested that she transfer to another school, but she said no, she would stick it out and finish the year.

She hung in there, fighting every step of the way. She had been dating a young man before she left and they kept up a correspondence. David, in his freshman year of college, was intrigued by what Elizabeth was learning and her passionate ambivalence toward it. When she called him at one point to say she was throwing in the towel and coming home, he said, "No, you're not. You love it too much. And you know something? I'm coming there to check this whole thing out myself!"

To his parents' chagrin, David took off a year from college and flew to Israel on a "fact-finding" mission. He ended up enrolling in Ohr Somayach Yeshivah. About a year later, he and Elizabeth became engaged. Back in the States, they faced strong opposition from David's parents, who disdained his religious lifestyle. It was a painful situation for the young couple: they had left a warm, supportive Torah environment in Israel, and were unsure of where to turn.

David's parents eventually asked me to meet with them. They came right to the point. They no longer opposed David's plans to continue learning in Israel, but wanted my support in talking the couple out of getting married until they had both finished college. Yes, it would mean waiting a few years, but that was the only practical route. The young couple had to be self-sufficient before starting out on their own, his mother said. Surely, we would agree!

At one time, I undoubtedly would have concurred. But I thought of my son who had turned away from Judaism just as I began to embrace it, and I thought of my fervent prayers that my other children would be able to find their place in the Jewish religion and learn to love the Torah. Here was the answer to that prayer staring me in the face and I was going to start bargaining and negotiating?

From deep down, a memory skimmed to the surface. Sunlight and stained glass. A little girl standing on tiptoe, gazing into the Holy Ark where exquisite Torah scrolls shimmer in the multi-colored light. "What are they?" she whispers in awe.

"These are Torah scrolls…G–d gave the Torah to the Jewish people," the elderly rabbi tells her. "That means it belongs to you and your family…"

"But who will support them?" David's mother was demanding. "Who will pay the rent, who will pay for food, clothing—what it takes to live?"

"We will," I heard someone say in a voice identical to mine. I looked around in astonishment and caught my husband's frown of disbelief at what I had just blurted out. It was one of those moments in life when something pushes you over the edge before you realize what is happening. But even while I trembled at the huge undertaking, my heart was bursting with pride.

&

Elizabeth and David moved to Israel after a joyous wedding that still seems like a fairy tale, Leona says. Rabbi Serebrowski, Rabbi Miller and other rabbis from Torah Links/Gesher were present, along with a large contingent of Lakewood friends whose happiness practically "set the place on fire." Rabbi Becher from Gateways, who had guided Elizabeth through the maze of confusing choices and questions to a year of inspiration and change in Israel, was a witness on the kesubah *and under the* chupah.

The couple lives in Maalot Dafne, a short distance from Ohr Somayach where David is learning. Occupying an honored place on their dining room wall is their wedding picture: chosson *and* kallah *under the* chupah, *smiling parents in the background, and the* mesader kedushin, *Rabbi Matisyahu Solomon of Lakewood, pronouncing the* brachos.

Last Chance

Ruth's Story

What would you do if your daughter showed up at your house one day with her seventh-month-old-baby and said, "Ma, if you don't want her, I'm going to the welfare people. I can't deal with an infant at this point in my life."

I can't say we were shocked. The child's father was an alcoholic who had abandoned the family, and my daughter, Cynthia, was totally distraught. She simply wasn't coping. Sam and I took the baby temporarily, hoping our daughter would get her life back on track. But months went by and Cynthia gave no sign of wanting Pearl back. There was no room in her life for little Pearl.

When the child was two years old, I went to court to obtain legal custody. Cynthia willingly gave her up. After that, she came around from time to time to visit Pearl. She'd give her a little present and spend a few minutes playing with her. Then she'd sit in the living room and chat with us, puffing away on a cigarette. It didn't even register in her mind that smoke was like poison to my husband who had just had triple bypass surgery. I had to keep reminding her each time, as if she'd never heard this before.

After a while she'd be on her way, blowing a kiss to Pearl as she left. Sometimes I wanted to shake her. I wanted to say, "You had a mother who took care of you—why can't you do that for your own daughter? Why isn't she allowed to have what you had?"

From the time she started to talk, we could see Pearl was not an ordinary child. At three years old, she started to read. She'd move her tiny finger over the words in the picture book and read them softly to herself. We thought at first she had memorized the story, but then we saw she could read books no one had ever read to her.

By the age of five, she seemed to understand that it was hard for us to do many of the regular things that parents do for their kids. Sam and I both have serious health problems: Sam with his heart, and me with my thyroid. I also had a bout with cancer. We both take medication and most of the time we have very little energy.

When you're young and healthy, packing the kids into the car and zooming off to the store or to the park is no sweat. But those days are over for me. There are times in the morning when just getting out of bed is as draining as climbing a mountain.

You wouldn't think a six year old would understand something like this: her own mother showed so little sensitivity. But Pearl would try not to be a burden. She dressed herself, made her own breakfast, fixed her hair. Somehow, she sensed that our situation was not normal. Maybe she was worried about what would happen to her if we couldn't manage.

Because she was gifted, we wanted to find a private school for her that would help her develop her talents. We chose a new little school about a mile away from our home in Cherry Hill, New Jersey. It had a small student body and was supposed to be a very caring place. This was the Shalom Torah Academy.

I found out about it in the oddest way. I was carrying a bag of groceries to my car in the supermarket parking lot, when the bag ripped and everything spilled out. A young woman ran over to help me. She was so gracious and kind; we started talking. It turned out that she taught in the Academy.

Funny how little things like that point you in a certain direction. I ended up enrolling Pearl there even though, from a physical standpoint, the school was not impressive. The classes were held in a trailer, due to lack of space, and there was no lunchroom, gym, or library.

But there must have been something special going on inside that school. Pearl left the house each morning with such enthusiasm. She believed whatever her teachers taught her with her whole heart. If I had known the school was Orthodox right from the beginning, I would never have taken her there. I have my own history with Orthodox Judaism.

My grandfather was a Yiddish-speaking Polish immigrant who came to America in the early 1900s. He was ultra-Orthodox and the rabbi of a synagogue. I remember him as a grim man—almost never cracked a smile, even for his grandchildren. The entire family, even his married children, was under his control. He had five sons and four daughters and they were all afraid to disobey him.

One of the few memories I have of him is of a time one Friday night when we were supposed to go to my grandparents' house for the meal. I was about nine. On the way out, the button of my dress got caught on the door and ripped off. I wanted to sew it back on, but my mother said I can't because it's Shabbos. I said if I can't sew it on, I'm not going. I put up such a fuss that my mother didn't know what to do with me.

Finally, she took me into the bedroom, shut the door and quickly sewed the button back on. We got to my grandparents' house later than usual and I was terrified he would find out why. Every time he looked my way, I cringed. I was sure he could read my mind. The evening ended without incident, but I never forgot that fear that lay on my heart all evening.

But everyone loved my grandmother. We'd come on Friday after she lit the candles. She'd kiss everybody, give the children candy and ask us about school. After Grandma died, the joy went out of that house. My grandfather became even more severe. We stopped going there because there was nothing to go for anymore.

Right after he died, all nine children chucked the whole religion thing. They brought *treife* food into their homes; they went shopping or driving around on Shabbos; and what's more—they gloried in it. The way my mother described it to me, they felt like they'd been released from jail and were celebrating their freedom. So you can imagine what

Orthodoxy meant in our family as I was growing up.

When Pearl started coming home asking me to light candles Friday night, I balked. I wasn't ready to revisit my grandfather's world. But sweeter memories began to surface. I recalled that good feeling in Grandma's kitchen, with the Shabbos candles aglow. I remembered the special light in her eyes as she hugged and kissed us and gave us goodies. After all, Pearl's request was so small. If lighting candles on Friday night would give her the same feeling that once warmed my heart, why not?

When it came to keeping kosher, though, I drew the line. I was about to take her to eat out with Sam and me at Burger King one evening when she said to me, "But Grandma, we can't go to Burger King anymore." I said, "Sweetheart, you may not want to go. But don't tell me I can't, because I'm going. If you don't want to come with us, stay home and make yourself a sandwich." Of course, she came along. But she sat there very sad and quiet and didn't eat a thing.

I was convinced she was getting too deep into hard-core Judaism and I tried to talk her out of it. I said, "If you really want to be Orthodox, you have to do it all the way. You can't even watch TV on Shabbos; did you know that?" That hit her hard. I saw the doubt and confusion growing in her eyes.

You know those times in life when you do a really stupid thing and afterwards want to kick yourself for it? That's suddenly how I felt about what I'd said to Pearl. I said to myself, "Ruthie, you fool. What are you doing to this child? What are you proving, that you have the power to shatter her? The child comes running to you all excited about her new 25-cent diamond ring and you feel duty-bound to tell her it's fake?"

Pearl was seven by now. She was the most religious little girl you have ever seen. She made blessings before she ate anything and afterward, too. She begged me to buy her a skirt or two and a Shabbos dress so she wouldn't have to wear pants. She idolized Morah Basie and Morah Miri and wanted to be just like them.

All of this would have been aggravating except that she was also such an unusually kindhearted child. When I'd get one of my killer headaches, she'd rub my forehead, bring me ice, and try to be as quiet as a mouse. It baffled me how different she was from my daughter and from my son's two kids, who acted selfish and bad-mannered whenever they came around. Sometimes, I couldn't wait till they'd leave.

As crazy as it sounds, I felt that my own son, who was in his forties, was actually jealous of Pearl. It was obvious he didn't like her. He tried to tell us that raising her was too much of a strain on us, and we should give her away.

I often wondered—where did I go wrong with my own children? How did they turn out so cold-hearted? I'd look at little Pearl and think, "Please don't change, darling. Stay the way you are... you're my only hope. You're my last chance to do it right."

Maybe that's why we finally gave in and filled out the form she excitedly brought us from school one day. It was an application to a Gateways seminar. Pearl begged us to go and to take her along. My reaction was, "Not a chance." I gave the excuse that we can't afford it, but the truth was that I had no interest in spending my weekend being preached to by some Orthodox rabbis. It was enough having a little *rebbetzin* to deal with in my own home.

But she brought us her piggy bank and said we should empty it out and use the money for the seminar. She had maybe fifty dollars in there and her eyes were filled with such pleading. Sam and I looked at each other. We knew we'd lost.

Well, we signed up for the weekend and here comes the surprise. Gateways was better than Disney World, at least for Pearl. There was a children's program run by a team of counselors, and one of them was her Morah Miri. You wouldn't think a bunch of kids today could spend a full Saturday indoors without TV or fancy toys. But these counselors were amazing. I'd sneak over to watch what was going on in the children's room from time to time, and I finally understood why Pearl was so captivated by her teachers.

They loved her. You could see it in the way they spoke to her, how they smoothed her hair and held her hand. They, too, realized she was special.

For Sam and me, Gateways was a little bit like Disney World, too, in the sense of it being a little bit magical. They put a spin on Orthodox Judaism that made you feel like you had lived your entire life up to that point with blinders on. Where was this world when I was growing up, when my mother was growing up? All we knew of Judaism was a legacy of fear and grandfather's gloom.

Gateways showed us there is another world of Judaism. There was no pressure to be anything or do anything. They just wanted you to come with an open mind and hear what they had to say. They spoke about G–d as being as near to a human being as a parent to a child, and that the Torah is proof of how deeply interested He is in how we live our lives.

There was a strange moment when the thought flashed through my head that I had always thought of Judaism as my grandfather's religion, but it wasn't—it was G–d's! It wasn't meant to be harsh and forbidding. It was meant to teach people how to live in a way that would bring joy and love into a home. Somewhere along the line, people messed up and Orthodoxy got stuck with a terrible image it couldn't shake.

Towards the end of the seminar, a staff member came over to me. She introduced herself saying that she'd heard there was a grandparent here who had adopted her own granddaughter, and she wanted to meet the person who would do such a kindness. We wound up talking for over an hour. I found myself confiding in her about some of my health problems and Sam's heart condition, and how I was worried because Pearl had no one but us. What if something happened to us? No one in our small extended family would have the slightest interest in her. I choked up, unable to go on.

This woman just held my hand for a moment, without saying anything. Tears came to her eyes. "Talk it out with Hashem," she said finally. "He's the One to turn to. He can help you. He is your greatest friend in this world." For some reason, I believed her. Back home, I even tried her advice.

I know it sounds weird to people who have always been religious, but let me put it this way: Sam and I made a lot of friends by the time the seminar ended that Sunday. But there was one new Friend we had never known, a very special One, that we took all the way home with us…

Mid-Life
Crisis

Stephanie's Story

I thought my life had a fair amount of stability, even as a single parent. Good job, $75,000 a year with terrific benefits, my own home, a daughter I was crazy about, friends who cared. Absolute success would be finding the right guy to make this picture complete. I was optimistic, even though at 39, I should have been starting to worry.

I wasn't looking for any major changes in lifestyle and certainly not in religious outlook. What I was looking for, on one particularly rainy day in October, was a medical library. The daughter of a friend of mine had been diagnosed with a rare type of skin disorder, and I was looking for medical literature on the subject for her. I drove around Margate, New Jersey, for about a half an hour, trying to find the Center for Holistic Medicine, which was not where it should have been, according to the directions I had been given. So I finally parked and got out to make a phone call.

I was in some kind of community center, where people were milling around waiting for a meeting to start. I soon found out that the Center for Holistic Medicine had relocated to Cherry Hill, my own hometown, ten miles away! The woman who gave me this information pointed to a coffee machine inside the room where people were gathering, inviting me to partake before continuing on. I happened to be dying for a coffee at that moment, and I was touched by her hospitality. Over coffee, we struck up a conversation.

It turned out the meeting was a class on Judaism, on the topic of how to understand suffering from a Jewish viewpoint. Charlene, the woman I was speaking with, urged me to stay. "I can see the topic interests you," she ventured. I was already late for an appointment and declined. But on my way out of the building, I abruptly turned around and went back in. If there's someone walking around on this planet who can explain human suffering to me, I thought, I have to see who that is.

His name was Rabbi Ordman and his talk was about the search

for meaning in life. He spoke of how a worthy goal can change the worst pain into a labor of love. Listening to him, I forgot about my identity as an atheist. I felt the stirrings of an old hunger for a connection with something larger than a career; something larger than what I'm going to eat for dinner tonight; something that would give meaning to the trials I had gone through in my own life, especially in my childhood. The scars were still there.

The only Judaism I had in my life was a visit to a temple every Yom Kippur, which I dreaded. I remember that when my sister and I were very little, we were in a Jewish school for a short while. I liked it there. I felt that my teachers cared about me. I have some faint memories of the place... a sunny first grade classroom and a *mezuzah* on the side of the door that was too high for me to reach, even when I stretched up on tiptoe. I'd jump up and touch it with my hand to copy the taller kids who swiped it with their fingertips as they passed by, brushing those fingertips with a kiss afterward. I remember longing to be tall enough to kiss the *mezuzah* effortlessly.

I never got the chance. My father was unable to keep up the tuition payments and had too much pride to go before a board asking for charity. He took us all out and enrolled us in public school.

In retrospect, the class in Margate was the onset of a major upheaval in my life. I didn't see it coming and it kind of swept me away on high tide. Through some people I met at the class, I found out about the Gateways organization and attended one of their seminars. If you've ever been to one, you know what I mean about the psycho-energy of the lectures and the amazing feeling of being in a room with hundreds of Jews who are into Jewishness, maybe for the first time in their lives.

At one of the workshops at the seminar, people were talking about how the hectic pace of our lives keeps a person too dizzy to think. How I related to that! My job in a casino in Atlantic City is part of a lifestyle whose *very purpose* is to shut down a person's ability to think. It's a world that is devoted to keeping people from paying attention to anything but gambling and winning money. That's been my life and my social circle for twelve years. Can you imagine a more extreme contrast to a Jewish seminar about spirituality and G–dliness?

The seminar tempted me to learn more about what Judaism has to say about the purpose of life. One of the rabbis gave me some insight by describing Shabbos. He told us, "Shabbos is a time to stop playing G–d and try, instead, to spend time with Him." He explained the many restrictions of Shabbos as part of a regimen that had a single purpose: to free a person from the exhausting merry-go-round of weekday pursuits to spend time with G–d.

This appealed to me strongly. For the first time, I wanted to try this day of peace and rest. But then someone mentioned that cosmetics are off limits on Shabbos. This stopped me cold. I'm the type who doesn't put on lipstick once or twice a day. I put it on every hour. But I'm an absolutist. I don't believe in half-way measures. Lipstick was important to me, but if I'm taking the big view of things, do I let lipstick determine my destiny?

The question of what to do about Shabbos became a much bigger problem when I came back home. Saturday in a casino is peak business time. Nobody takes off on Saturday unless they're in a hospital in critical condition. And nobody, but nobody bucks casino rules. The corporation employs 30,000 people and they're ultra powerful. They'll blacklist anyone who crosses them.

When I finally got up the nerve and told them I wanted to stop working on Saturdays, they laughed in my face. They practically told me to get lost.

Well, I fought them and won—but I didn't do it alone. The Margate people and some rabbis in Lakewood—Rabbi Blech, Rabbi Gendelman and others—were fighting along with me. They put me in touch with an expert in labor law, a top attorney for whom people have to wait for months before getting a consultation with him. They even got the Agudah organization involved because of the issue of religious freedom in the workplace. Every door in the Jewish community was open to me to help me win the right to keep my job without working on Shabbos.

Once, as I was on a conference call planning strategy with the labor law expert and two other rabbis, it hit me that it was after midnight! These people, whose lives were so busy, were conferencing with me at such a crazy hour because of a principle that was larger than any one of us. Absolutely no one in my world would be able to fathom the importance of this. I felt so lucky to be a part of it.

I was astonished by how Jews pull together to help each other, the incredible outreach to a stranger. Rabbi Suchard from Gateways kept in regular touch with me and gave me tremendous moral support. The Gateways staff arranged Shabbos invitations for me and invited me to a class they had organized in Lakewood on "The Power of the Tongue," based on an English version of a book by the Chofetz Chaim.

A few weeks ago, I experienced a serious accident and this book played a very critical role in my life. I was at a friend's house and wanted to take a short nap before driving home. I removed my lenses and put them into wetting solution, got comfortable on the couch and went to sleep. Afterwards, driving home, my eyes started to burn as though they were on fire. I barely made it home, almost passing out from the pain. I managed to call an ambulance, but by the time it arrived, I couldn't see anymore. The paramedic took the bottle of "wetting solution" I had used and examined the label. It was peroxide. Suddenly they were rushing me out the door on a stretcher and shouting instructions.

I was stunned by the realization that I'd gone blind. My mind churned in agony, picturing my desolate future—a sightless woman with no job, dependent on others for the smallest thing, a pathetic creature.

The book on the power of the tongue that I'd been learning in the Lakewood class was on the coffee table. Sobbing, I asked the paramedic to find it and please bring it along. "Do you think you'll be needing it?"

he asked gently.

"Please, I need it!" I cried out. He got it for me. I held it close to me in the ambulance and kept it in my arms in the emergency room while I was being examined. I wouldn't let them take it from me.

I don't know how to read Hebrew and never learned to pray. But in the few months that I had been exposed to religious Jews, I'd learned to say "*Baruch Hashem.*" I held this book tightly and poured my agony and despair and pleading to G–d in those two words. "*Baruch Hashem* – Please, *Hashem! Baruch Hashem*—Please, *Hashem*, please help me!" I sobbed over and over again.

Look into my eyes, now, four weeks later. What do you see? It's utterly miraculous. The cornea and retina in both eyes are 98% healed. When they took off the bandages and I could see images right away, I broke down in tears. My doctor was astounded. He wasn't used to being speechless, but he could think of absolutely nothing to say. He finally said, "Stephanie, the damage to the retina should have been permanent after contact with something so corrosive. I can't explain what happened here! Consider yourself a very lucky woman."

I blubbered, "Doctor, luck has nothing to do with it. It's a miracle from heaven, don't you see that?" He just smiled, shaking his head in bewilderment.

❧

Stephanie left Atlantic City as soon as she fully recovered. She moved with her daughter to a Jewish community near Lakewood where she works as an interior decorator. She keeps in close contact with the friends she made at Gateways and her new connections in Lakewood.

"You Want
Me To Do
WHAT?"

Margaret's Story

I was a Reform Jew married to a man who started out Conservative, but was increasingly drawn to Torah beliefs. We were in such different places spiritually that we had to get married in his backyard; Josh refused to step into my Reform temple and I wouldn't go to his *shul*.

My aversion to an Orthodox *shul* was not merely the result of being unable to read or understand a word of Hebrew. It had to do with the *mechitzah*: seeing the women seated behind the partition made me physically ill. The sense of hurt and injustice I felt—that women were not permitted to be visible—was so strong it brought me to tears.

The ongoing tug of war over our divergent religious paths continued for many years, as Josh began to embrace additional aspects of Jewish observance—a trend I tried my best to fight off. Our "mixed marriage" held together under the enormous strain only by a miracle. In addition to being committed to each other, we became very adept at negotiating and making compromises.

There was another factor: While Josh's insistence on bringing religion into our home made me angry enough to want to eat a cheeseburger right in front of him, I knew one thing: to him, Judaism was not a control issue or a "you lose-I win" contest. It was a matter of conscience. Knowing that took the edge off my rage.

The issues we fought over were about keeping kosher, Shabbos and the Jewish holidays. I saw the Orthodox laws as stifling anachronisms, utterly lacking in relevance and meaning in today's world.

Beyond this rational argument, there was an emotional one: in my world, those practices were downright embarrassing. Looking too Jewish, behaving too Jewish was considered bad manners, even somewhat shameful.

Take Passover. My folks knew how to have a Seder. We followed the instructions in a small booklet put out by the Reform movement called "The Concise 20-Minute Seder." If you followed the manual, you could be assured of a Seder that would be over in no more than half an hour.

But Josh was learning more about Passover rituals, and would have none of this quickie business. So we argued about how we could observe the Seder to Josh's satisfaction while still being spared a long and tedious affair in which I had absolutely no interest.

Then came the biggest storm of all—Josh's request that I keep "the laws of family purity," something I had never heard of, but darkly assumed would be stifling and puritanical. He launched into a summary of what it involved. I stopped him cold. "You want me to do *what?*" I exclaimed in disbelief. I drew a line right there. I didn't care what this rabbi or that rabbi had to say. No one was going to railroad me into any more nonsense.

I felt that too many concessions had already been wrung from me. Each time we had wrangled over a religious matter, I had drawn a line in the sand, only to let myself be dragged across it.

For example, after hours of debate, I had grudgingly agreed to keep kosher in the house (on condition that I could eat what I pleased outside the house.) The next surrender was over lighting Shabbos candles. I finally agreed to do so, but only whenever I felt like it.

In deference to Josh, we even had a special Friday night Shabbos dinner —whenever I happened to finish cooking it. After endless negotiating, I even agreed not to drive on Shabbos, except to drive to my temple for services, which I did without the slightest compunction.

When the issue of the family purity laws came up, I felt rebellion brewing in me. I had already lost enough ground. Josh's brand of Judaism was beginning to feel like a guest who has not only overstayed his welcome, but has made himself a royal pain in the neck.

Yet it was clear that Josh had drawn his own line in the sand. Realizing once again that, for him, ignoring these ritual laws was an unbearable violation of conscience, forced me to a crossroads.

Logically, I should have turned down a suggestion that came shortly after this impasse from the rabbi of Josh's *shul*. Rabbi Feldheim was connected with Gateways, a Jewish outreach organization that sponsored Jewish seminars and retreats in the tri-state area. The rabbi urged us to attend, saying we would learn more about Judaism at one Gateways seminar than most Jews learn in a lifetime.

Despite my distaste for his Orthodox beliefs, I knew Rabbi Feldheim was a sincere person: but his claim that there was so much more for me to learn about Judaism rang hollow. As a teacher of comparative religions, I was more informed about Judaism than most people I knew. I was skeptical that a seminar on Judaism could teach me much.

I thanked the rabbi politely, handing back the brochure, saying, "It looks interesting, but we just can't afford it." A couple of days later, he called us with the news that he'd spoken to the Gateways people and they had offered us an attractive discount.

I felt cornered. I knew the weekend would be a waste of my time, but I had trouble saying no. Deep down, I suspected I was being less than intellectually honest. Could I really claim to be an expert on Judaism? I was familiar with Reform, Conservative, and Reconstructionist ideologies, but Orthodoxy so irked me, I found every excuse to avoid studying it. When I taught comparative religions, I glossed right over it.

In the end, I relented and we drove with our two kids from Philadelphia to the seminar in New Jersey. Josh was in a buoyant mood all the way, in counterpoint to my tired resignation. As we pulled up to the hotel, I braced myself for a heavy dose of Jewish fundamentalism. It's just for a weekend, I thought grimly. I can get through a weekend.

One of the very first lectures asked me to consider the possibility that the Torah was G–d-given. I had never before given the notion that G–d dictated the laws to Moses the slightest credence. But the speaker, Rabbi Suchard, pointed out something intriguing. He quoted some of the Torah's explicit promises and guarantees that defy the laws of nature, but which nevertheless all materialized in the course of history.

He emphasized the prophecies that foretell the exile of the Jewish people to all four corners of the world for not obeying the Torah's commandments. Other verses foretold the Jewish nation's indestructibility. Instead of fading into oblivion over centuries of exile and persecution, the Jewish people would miraculously endure.

All the expulsions and holocausts that decimated this chosen people would nevertheless fail to destroy them, the Torah promised.

Was it mere coincidence that these prophecies have come true? Or could it be that the One who made these promises knew precisely what would occur centuries ahead of their happening—and in fact guided world events in this direction?

The speaker quoted some lines from an obscure letter by Mark Twain that made chills run down my spine:

"The Egyptian, the Babylonian, and the Persian rose, filled the planet with sound and splendor, then faded to dream-stuff and passed away; the Greek and the Roman followed, and made a vast noise, and they are gone. Other peoples have sprung up and held their torch high for a time, but it burned out, and they sit in twilight now, or have vanished.

"The Jew saw them all, beat them all, and is now what he always was, exhibiting no decadence ... no dulling of his alert and aggressive mind. All things are mortal but the Jew; all other forces pass, but he remains. What is the secret of his immortality?"

"Could it be," the rabbi asked, "that the secret of the Jewish people's immortality is, very simply, that the Creator of the world promised it would be so, and kept His promise?"

This was a massive leap of faith by any standard, I thought to myself. But the proverbial rug had been yanked from beneath my feet. *My G–d*, I caught myself thinking, *what if he's right?*

By the end of the seminar, I was beginning to understand why Orthodox Jews cling so stubbornly to the Torah's laws, even those which seem so rigid and antiquated. They were trying to uphold what to them is a sacred legacy in the face of the world's scorn. I know all about Orthodox-bashing. I came from there.

In the deeply assimilated milieu where I had grown up, my family would have been happier had I married a Christian instead of an observant Jew like Josh. Judaism was something to be hidden away in shame. Thinking about my siblings and Josh's, almost all of whom had married Christians, I now understood how their brand of Judaism would self-destruct in a matter of one or two generations.

I also began to understand how Jewish survival was impossible without Jewish pride and education. To make a long story short, Gateways launched me on a journey of discovery into a realm I had never dreamed I'd want to explore.

With the help of the staff, I hooked up via telephone with some knowledgeable women in different places across the country. We have learning sessions, one-on-one, once a week. With one "partner," I learn the laws of Shabbos; with another, the meaning of the prayers; and with a third, topics from the weekly *parshah*.

I still can't pray using a *siddur*. But with the help of Rabbi Feldman, our home is *glatt* kosher. Over a period of several months, I began to dress more in keeping with the laws of modesty. Sometimes, looking in the mirror, I can barely recognize myself. And yes, those laws of family purity that meant so much to Josh – they're on my list too.

I quit the Reform temple right before Rosh Hashanah. This was a very difficult move for me. I enjoyed the services and had a whole network of friends there. I was considered among the more knowledgeable members, in contrast to Josh's synagogue, where I stand out as an ignoramus. I would be less than honest if I said I didn't miss the temple, the people, and my activities there.

But as I get into my new life, I feel more and more in sync with it. Even the *mechitzah* no longer aggravates me… as much. Mrs. Greenblatt, an instructor at Gateways, helped me shift my perception. "The way you feel about the *mechitzah* flows from your purpose in going to synagogue," she said. "Ask yourself why you're there. Is it to interact with people or to connect with G–d?

"Imagine prayer as a desperately-sought interview with an important head of state. Now your appointment has finally arrived. Are you going to blow it by paying attention to distractions and forgetting your carefully prepared petition? If the goal is to connect with G–d, the *mechitzah* can only facilitate that by giving men and women the privacy and space they need to concentrate on a very important opportunity."

In my old temple, I have to admit, prayer was on the agenda, but it was hardly the focus. With young, attractive women singing and leading services, often dressed provocatively, the electricity in the air was not necessarily spiritual.

Shabbos has become a pivotal family encounter. My two little boys love everything about this day, from the Friday afternoon aroma of challah baking in the oven to the excitement of Shabbos guests and special foods and treats. For me, walking to shul together as a family is one of the simple but beautiful highlights of the day.

My biggest challenge is trying to mend the broken fences in my relationship with my parents. It's painful for all of us. No matter how I present it, they feel that in becoming religious, I've rejected not only their values, but *them*. And the wall they have erected between us hurts no one more than the grandchildren they waited so long to have.

I can picture the next time they visit. My seven-year-old Larry will zoom past them on his bike, waving gaily. They're about to smile back when they catch sight of his *tzitzis* flying in the wind. The smile turns to a frown. Larry's waving hand freezes and drops to his side. What did he do to anger them, he wonders sadly.

"Look what she's doing to those poor kids!" My parents moan to each other. "How will they get anywhere in life? What a pity!"

I swallow hard. I love the sight of my son's *tzitzis*, but just a short while ago I was reading my parents' script to Josh. So who am I to judge them or complain? When I say the morning blessing, "Blessed are You, G–d, for opening the eyes of the blind," I ask Hashem to lift the darkness from them as He did for me.

I never asked Josh, but I'm sure that must have been his number one prayer all the years he struggled to help me see the light.

From The
Land of the
Living

Judah's Story

My father was killed in a car accident when I was ten years old. The tragedy left an open wound in me that in some ways never healed. Even 30 years later, part of me was still mourning him.

As a teenager I'd go to the cemetery on the anniversary of his death and brood about how different my life would be had my father lived. I was angry and in despair over being orphaned. My mother was overwhelmed by the problems of raising five rambunctious boys on her own. I couldn't turn to her with my problems.

Mom's parents were from Latvia. They came over before the war, sometime in the 1920s. They kept an Orthodox home and tried to pass their traditions on to their children, but my mother and her siblings drifted away from religion as soon as they left home.

In my own family, we kept a few mementos of Judaism: we dutifully lit Chanukah candles and celebrated Passover with a family feast, but that was it. I went to Sunday school for Hebrew lessons before my bar mitzvah but I made so much trouble there, they expelled me.

After my father's death, my mother threw herself into charity work and other activities sponsored by the Conservative temple to which our family belonged. She seemed to find solace being around the synagogue, and urged my brothers and me to attend services.

We always wormed our way out of going. I had no interest in a G–d who broke my heart by taking away my father. In a span of 30 or so years after my bar mitzvah, I walked into a synagogue maybe five times, not including High Holidays.

It was after my divorce that I took a second look at Jewish observance. I had moved to Long Island from Detroit with my two daughters after the breakup, realizing we needed to be close to family. I listened with a mixture of amusement and exasperation as my mother revived her campaign to get me involved in the synagogue.

"Judah, how about meeting the rabbi?" she began. "They need members like you—responsible, reliable—a family man. You'll like each other. There's so much you can do to help build up the temple."

"No thanks, Mom. I am not going to have my life revolve around religion," I told her. "You ought to know me well enough to know that's not the answer for me."

She tried a different tack. "Well, don't you at least want to find out what school options you have for the kids? Rabbi Neuman has connections to Jewish schools. He can help you."

"Mom," I groaned. "I can't afford the tuition at those private schools."

"I'll help you with tuition, Judah. This is important. The public schools here are very low-standard."

I knew she was right. My twin girls had been in a day school back in Detroit and it wouldn't be fair to put them into a public school environment at this point. They'd had enough upheavals in their lives.

With Rabbi Neuman's help, I enrolled Laurie and Dara in a Conservative day school. Mom must have a streak of clairvoyance. The rabbi and I became friendly. Not only did I end up becoming a member of his synagogue, two years later, I became the president.

At the time, I felt that taking a leadership role in the synagogue was a major step forward in religious commitment, since it obliged me to keep the basics of Shabbos and *kashrus*.

It soon became obvious, though, that this was my own naïve take on things. Far from being expected of me, my move toward religious observance impressed or pleased no one. In a place where the vast majority of members were not interested in coming to services or keeping *any* religious rituals, it was barely noted.

Most of the members were content with wearing the Conservative badge while living a Reform lifestyle. Getting a *minyan* together for Friday night and Shabbos morning services was a weekly headache. Besides Rabbi Neuman and myself, there were just three or four regulars. This, in spite of a dues-paying membership of 800 people!

With a whole range of exciting activities to compete with on Saturday—going to the movies, golfing, shopping, sleeping late, eating out, the beach in the summertime, Little League in the spring, football in the fall…How surprising was it that Sabbath services couldn't muster a following?

It was demoralizing. People just weren't interested in what we were selling! And truthfully, I couldn't blame them. I, too, was confused about the relevance of a religion summed up by holiday parties and folklore; a religion that didn't relate to G–d.

Whatever the reason for its lack of appeal, any program that couldn't attract even one percent of its members to Sabbath services was in deep trouble. I thought seriously about quitting, although I hated to walk out on Rabbi Neuman.

By now, the twins were teenagers and Dara, who had become friends with some religious girls at a Jewish Education Program (JEP) Shabbaton, was invited by them to help out in the children's program at a Gateways seminar. She came back glowing with excitement about the girls she had met there and the kind of classes the seminar ran.

"Dad, you ought to think about signing up for the next one. It's the kind of thing you'd like," she said.

"What would I like about it?" I probed.

"It's like, really amazing," she said with typical adolescent articulateness.

"Amazing, huh?"

"Yeah, here's a brochure. You can see from the topics."

My eye ran down the list of lectures: *Fingerprints of Divinity... The Greatest Claim Ever Made: Revelation at Sinai...* Intrigued, I followed up on Dara's suggestion and, a couple of months later, all three of us went to a Gateways seminar. Dara was right. The weekend was truly stimulating. I was amazed that "fundamentalist Judaism" could be so persuasive.

Kashrus was a Divine commandment, not a quaint leftover from a primitive culture, they argued. One lecture showed how modern science had shed light on why kosher slaughter was the most humane way of killing a cow, using recently discovered facts about a cow's anatomy that differed from the anatomy of other animals. At the time that all the *kashrus* laws were coded over two millennia ago, the speaker pointed out, whom but G–d could have known such a thing?

For a long time after that weekend, I wrestled with a desire to explore Judaism further as the literal word of G–d. But I sensed that going down this road would bring me into too much conflict with the way I had set up my life with my children. Finally, with mixed feelings, I made plans to attend a President's Day Weekend retreat.

I was listening to one of the final lectures of the weekend which delved into the Jewish concept that life continues after death. Rabbi Suchard stressed that one of the only ways a soul can be elevated after it leaves this world is through the good deeds performed in memory of the departed.

"The souls of those who have passed on know the truth about Hashem and His Torah," he said. "But they can do nothing with this knowledge. Their time is over. Only we, in the land of the living, can help them earn merit."

The rabbi went on to relate a story* [found in *The Maggid Speaks*, by Rabbi Pesach Krohn] of a secular Israeli family who had moved to America, only to lose their father in a tragic road accident. The grief-stricken mother returned to Israel with her two children. In search of solace, she attended a Discovery Seminar, which opened up a world she had never known. Slowly she began to draw closer to religious observance. She withdrew her children from public school and transferred them to a yeshivah.

Due to his lack of background, her son, Ami, had difficulty keeping up with his classmates. The child went to bed in tears one night after confiding to his mother that he could not understand the Gemara and was sure to fail the test the following morning.

When he awoke the next morning, however, he was in much better spirits. His mother offered to write a note to the *rebbe* explaining that her son needed more time to review the material; but Ami said it wasn't necessary.

"I had a wonderful dream," he told his mother. In his dream, he saw his father, who hugged him close. "Abba, do you know that we are now religious?" the overjoyed child asked his father. His father said he knew.

"The day Ima brought you to yeshivah, I was allowed into *Gan Eden*," he told the boy.

Ami confided that learning Talmud was very hard for him in his new school. "It will get easier, Ami," his father said. "Do you know something? Here in *Shamayim*, we are learning the same thing you are. That's because whatever Torah you learn in this world, I am allowed to learn here."

"Then can you teach it to me, Abba? I have no one to help me with it," Ami said sadly. "Yes, Ami, we'll learn it together," his father said.

"Abba explained the Gemara to me and answered all my questions," the boy told his mother happily.

"My Ami got a hundred on his test," the mother later confided to friends, wiping tears from her cheeks.

As I listened to this story, the floodgates started to open. *I was that young boy!* For years after my father died, I felt a big hole in my heart. I longed to see him again, to feel his love, to feel connected. If only I had known that in the World of Truth, *it was he who needed me!*

I made it to my room, overcome by the realization. "Dad," I cried in my heart, "I didn't know! It took me decades to figure it out. But at least I know now what I have to do."

After I composed myself, I went over to Rabbi Suchard and said to him simply, "I'm ready, Rabbi." We spoke for a long time. He grasped that I was ready to do something concrete about bringing learning and observance into my life. Later, he introduced me to Rabbi Labrie at the Mesorah Foundation in Long Island. Under his guidance, I embarked on an intense journey into the world of learning.

It was a rigorous five-day a week, crack-of-dawn program. For six months, I got up at 5:30 in the morning, drove a half hour to the Mesorah Foundation, *davened* and then sat down to learn with Rabbi Labrie or Rabbi Katz for an hour or two. Sometimes I came back at night for another session.

We studied the laws of Shabbos, *Gemara* and topics in *mussar*. At times, driving back home I was so tired, I had to pull over to the side and close my eyes for a few minutes. At work, I'd sometimes find myself dozing off. But I had a lifetime of catching up to do and I was determined to make a dent in it.

That summer, I sent my two daughters to a camp run by JEP, closed my business temporarily and flew to Israel, where I enrolled in Ohr Somayach. I took an apartment in Sanhedria and spent my entire day in the yeshivah, from 9:00 in the morning until 9:00 at night. It was a magical time. I was living in a bubble, far from the "real" world.

As the summer ended, I felt I was returning home a different person. I was nervous about how to pick up the threads of my previous life. How would my daughters react to some changes I wanted to make in our home? Some things, like higher standards in *kashrus*, wouldn't be a problem. But raising our standards in other areas like Shabbos would be harder. I worried about this all the way home. My relationship with my children was the most important thing in my life. I didn't want to create conflict in our home.

After landing, on the way back, I did something I had been longing to do. I drove to the cemetery in Queens where my father is buried. I said *Tehillim* at his grave and stood there thinking about the twists and turns my life had taken. I asked Hashem to help me work things out in a way that would bring my father *nachas* in the World of Truth.

Coming home, I found a letter from one of my daughters that brought tears to my eyes. She and her sister had reached a decision over the summer. They had both decided that they wanted to transfer to an Orthodox high school in the fall.

"Open for me the eye of a needle," G-d tells us, "and I will create an opening for you as wide as a palace entrance..." I imagined my daughter's letter fluttering down from the Heavens with a little post-it note attached, saying "Blessings from Above."